D1377847

AFRICA, O AFRICA

AFRICA,
O AFRICA

By
Louise Robinson Chapman

*Twenty years a missionary on the dark
continent*

Printed in U.S.A.
1945

BEACON HILL PRESS
2923 Troost Avenue, Kansas City, Missouri

DEDICATION
TO
FAIRY,
MY
FRIEND

CONTENTS

FOREWORD

Africa, O Africa! I cannot remember the time when Africa first put her hand upon me. It seems I have always been a part of her, and she a part of me. As a young girl I saw her in my dreams, and in the visions of my waking hours. Her people called to me from the darkness. She put out her hand and plucked me from my friends. Through twenty years of missionary life that grip never loosened. Africa never lost her attractiveness for me. Her lovable people left a deep imprint upon my life. Experience has built many memories—memories of happy association with fellow missionaries whom I love as my own brothers and sisters; memories of long friendships with native sons and daughters of Africa. The print of Africa's hand is upon me, and shall be to the end of my days.

I am dedicating this book to Fairy Chism, who was my college roommate and dearest friend. We lived and preached together in America until I went to Africa in 1920. When she came to Africa in 1928 she was stationed with me, and we lived and worked together until I left the field at the end of 1940.

Fairy was always devout and sacrificial, possessed with both natural and divine grace. A woman of prayer and faith and tremendous zeal. I think of her in both the mode of saint and that of a cheerful, happy, refreshing colaborer. Many were the victories God gave us as we worked together, and many people spoke our names as though we were really just one person.

I recall many serious and many amusing incidents regarding Fairy. When she came to Africa, she was determined to learn the Zulu language. She fairly ate and slept with her grammar. But at Christmas time she shut herself up in her hut to fast and pray and ask God for the gift of the Zulu tongue. After she had missed several meals, I went down to find the cause of her fast, thinking that she might be lonesome or homesick. At first she would not tell me what was on her mind. But when I refused to leave until she did tell, she finally stood out in the middle of her hut, and with streaming eyes, and dramatic motioning of her hands, cried, "I am tired of doing nothing and of saying nothing. God gave people the gift of language on the day of Pentecost, and I have determined to have the gift of Zulu before I leave this hut." But Fairy was always sane, and I soon convinced her that if she would faithfully study the language, the customs, and the people themselves, that by the time she knew enough about the people to be able to bring God's message to them, she would be able to speak. And God did give her the language in this way, and she became very proficient.

Came Fairy's first attempt to preach in Zulu. She used the text, "The day of the Lord so cometh as a thief in the night" (I Thessalonians 5:2). But the word for coming down is very much like the one for coughing, and the word for thief is very similar to the one for wild beast. After closing her Bible, Fairy confused these words, and, being limited in Zulu vocabulary, she quoted her text over and over again, saying with great earnestness, "The day of the Lord is coughing like a wild beast in the night." A coughing wild beast in the night is a dreadful picture to a Swazi child, and the sight of those little Africans listening to their missionary telling them of what is coming remains with me yet. I told Fairy she should have called an altar service, for surely when the Lord begins to cough like a wild beast in the night, it is time for little Swazi children to repent.

A Dutch farmer asked Fairy to pull his aching tooth, and with a straw he pointed out the offending member. Fairy hitched on, and after a bit the tooth came out. The man held his face for a moment, and then said, "I'm glad to have that one out, but, now, please get the one that is aching."

Fairy stuck her finger into a hole in the big kerosene lamp to get the glue off of it. Then the finger would not come out. Pulling and soaping did not avail. Everywhere that Fairy went the lamp was sure to go. Carl Mischke was at Endingeni at the time, and he cut the lamp to shreds with huge tin shears. Fairy does not put her finger into lamps any more.

Fairy wanted to ride my mule, Coffee. I was afraid for her, but finally consented when she promised to be very careful, and to hold the reins tight. I came just in time to see her prepare to mount. She was so interested in saying good-by to the natives that she left the reins loose, and I saw Coffee just ready to take a nip out of her back. Fairy saw too—the mule with teeth bared and ears flat. She went over toward him and said, "Coffee, you naughty mule." Coffee lifted his hind foot, put it in Fairy's stomach, and landed her over in the middle of a bamboo bush. I ran to help her, but she came out laughing, and said, "Dulile, you should have seen how funny you looked when I was going into that bush." Her own narrow escape did not impress her.

Fairy had a little lamb. She got it from a sheep farmer. It drank up all our milk, followed her to school and all through the house, parked in my office and ate up all the house plants, but when it devoured a bed of carnations all the household got up in arms and Fairy gave the little sheep to another farmer. Then she got Joco, a little monkey. He cleaned his teeth with a brush, picked pins out of Fairy's hair and went to school. Friends made him a little red suit and cap of which he was very proud. He was a real delight, and a great torment, and finally became such a pest that he—well, disappeared.

A representative of the King of England visited Swaziland during the time we were building the girls' home. The message of his coming went astray, so the distinguished guest with all the high officials of Swaziland arrived at the mission unannounced. It was Saturday morning. Fairy had been working in the garden with the girls. Her clothes and shoes were covered with dirt, and she decided to wash her hair before she changed. As she was finishing the process, her guests arrived, and found her in most unlovely attire. She sent them up to the new buildings, a few hundred yards from our old quarters, and ran into the house, brushed her wavy hair, gave it one twist, grabbed her best shoes and hose, donned a pretty yellow ruffled dress, ran up another trail, beat the visitors to the new building, and stood on the porch to receive them, looking like a fairy. The party stopped dead still as though they had seen an apparition. Then the honored guest said, feelingly, "That's the quickest change I ever saw." Everybody laughed, and years later when someone visited England and saw this man, the only Swazilander he asked about was the little missionary girl who made the quick change.

I have tried to tell things as I saw them and knew them in Africa. I hold my colaborers and the present missionary force of our field in the highest esteem, and ascribe to them credit for the great work they have done individually and as a force. Some of them have seen phases of the work that I did not see, and if they should write a book, it would differ in many respects from mine, and yet all would be true, for facts within themselves cannot speak, but must depend for voice upon those who see and know them. This is my excuse and apology.

LOUISE ROBINSON CHAPMAN.

PART ONE—PERSONAL EXPERIENCES

My Conversion

I was born in a one-room log cabin in a pioneer community in Clarke County, Washington. Our cabin was soon exchanged for a new house made of home-split shingles and hewed timbers. Here our family lived during my early childhood, with no Sunday school or church house in the whole neighborhood.

When I was about to finish high school, my father bought a new farm near View, Washington, and I went out to visit him, and to see our new property. There was a little church in this neighborhood, and I went on Sunday morning to hear the young people sing. Being a little late, I had to take the one empty seat up in the front pew. That morning I heard for the first time testimonies from hearts filled with the joy of God. Little Grandma Hansen jumped up and down in the aisle and shouted the praises of God. Mother Coatney had been passing through deep sorrow. She did not testify with words, but she smiled and kept looking up as though she could see someone above her. I had never seen such a look of rest and peace. I wondered what she had about which to smile. A voice in my heart whispered, "If you had what she has, you could smile too."

I well remember two songs they sang. One was:
"I was so lonely, so very lonely,
    When out in the desert I wandered alone."

13

The other was:

"Will you come? will you come? there is mercy for
   you,
   Balm for your aching breast;
Only come as you are, and believe on His name;
   Jesus will give you rest."

I felt sinful and distressed, and might have accepted
Jesus that day, but something seemed to tell me that
if I followed Christ, I would have some few things to
straighten up with people. I had never heard of restitution, but it seemed reasonable and right that one
who wanted to make peace with God should also make
peace with man. When I thought of how humiliating
this would be, I became very angry with myself, and
with everybody else. I had entered the church that
morning proud and contented. I came out miserable
and unhappy. For weeks after I went back to school,
conviction grew until I could neither eat nor sleep. I
was afraid to be alone, and thought I could hear
those people praying for me. I was burdened with
sin and afraid of God.

One night I tried to pray, but again I remembered
my troubles with people, and decided I would rather
die unsaved than to humiliate myself by asking anyone
to forgive me. Such darkness and hopelessness took
hold of my soul that, finally, after a desperate struggle,
I promised God that at the first opportunity I would approach these people and accept all the blame for our
differences. I supposed I would have to go back to the
praying people at the church before I could find salva-

tion; so I promised God I would go as soon as possible, and there make a public confession. Fear left my heart but no joy came.

A few weeks later I went back to the neighborhood of the church and found that the Elliott brothers were holding a protracted meeting in a little country schoolhouse eight miles from View. I sat by the door with the young people. I do not remember a word that was preached or a song that was sung. I did not feel as I did that first day, but was afraid to break the promise I had made to God. I had come to go to the altar, and I expected that God was going to meet me there. As soon as the sermon was ended, I left my friends and went to the altar alone. I did not know how to pray, but Christ met me there almost as soon as I knelt down. I knew something had taken place within my heart. I was no longer afraid of God. Rest, peace and assurance filled my soul.

Next morning at home, while washing clothes in the back yard, unspeakable joy suddenly filled my whole being. I forgot that people might see me, and I ran up and down the yard shouting and singing. I thought that day all life would thereafter be one great day of joyful emotion.

My Growing Concern for Others

I felt that the Lord wanted me to spend the summer at home. I went out into the pasture each day to pray. My heart was overflowing with joy and victory. I prayed for myself, and praised God for His blessings on my life. Those were wonderful days. Then other evangelists came for a meeting, and Rev. Earnest Matthews preached on grace before meals and family prayer. Then God said to me, "I want you to return thanks at your father's table, and establish a family altar in your home." I was frightened. I was sure I could not do it, and did not think it reasonable that God should ask me for such difficult service so early in my Christian walk. There was a bitter struggle, but I saw that if I was to keep the joy of salvation, I must obey God, so one night, with my head in the straw under the altar at the meeting, I decided that with God's help, I would perform even this hard task; and promised that I would begin the very next morning.

Before breakfast the next morning, members of the family became cross, and it seemed a most inopportune time to begin, but I felt the supporting arm of God about me, and found strength to thank God for His provision for our needs before the whole family. At family prayer, I read just one verse, "Let not your hearts be troubled. Ye believe in God, believe also in me." I stammered a few short sentences, and the worst was over. After this experience I prayed for myself and for my people. That year both my parents, and others of the family were saved.

One night the following winter, just as I was about to go to sleep, a great burden came upon my soul for Roy Davis, a neighbor boy who was very ill and unsaved. I prayed for Roy all night. At ten minutes to four in the morning great rest and assurance came to my heart. I knew God had heard my prayer, and

was assured that Roy would make his peace with
God. At four that morning, just ten minutes after
God gave me assurance that my prayer was heard,
Roy died unexpectedly, without having opportunity
to talk with anybody. I was so glad I had obeyed God,
and had prayed for Roy. I saw then that my friends
needed my prayers, so my vision was enlarged, and
after that I prayed for myself, my family and my
friends.

One Sunday afternoon I went to the pasture to
pray. I was so happy that I stayed all afternoon. In
the evening I thought I heard the footfall of many people, and I looked up to see who might be going through
our pasture. I saw what seemed to be a very long
cement street. Its windowless walls reached up to
heaven. I could hear many running footsteps, but
could see nothing but the empty street. As I drew
closer, I began to see forms. Suddenly I saw these
forms clearly. There were many, many people of
every age and size; people of every color from every
tribe and nation. I looked long at a beautiful woman
clothed in red velvet. She was refined and educated.
She ran swiftly, and gazed fixedly ahead. By her side
ran a dark-skinned heathen man clothed in one
scanty animal skin. His hair was full of red clay, his
uplifted hand grasped a club. His naked, greasy
shoulder rubbed against the beautiful shining gown
of the refined woman as they ran side by side. She did
not see him, and he did not see her. All ran at a mad
pace, every eye fixed ahead. No one seemed to see

or hear anyone else. I called to them and asked them
why they ran so fast, and where they were going, but
no one looked or answered a word. I pushed up the
line, and finally saw that this cement street was the
path of life, and that this running multitude was the
people of this world who must needs go down this
way, since there were no openings through which one
might escape. Satan stood at the far end of the passage
lashing the people so that those from the rear pressed
upon those ahead, and caused them to run yet faster
and ever faster. I turned about and ran down the way
of life until I came to a horrible pit into which the
people were falling. Their eyes were still fixed and
glassy, and not until their feet slipped over the edge
of hell did they awaken. Then, too late, they began
to cry for help. I tried to save them, but they were
pushed on by the ever-coming multitudes. I screamed
for them to stop. I pleaded, I begged, but they seemed
not to hear. I remembered Christ, and hastened back
to the spot where He had talked with me before I saw
the people. While yet a long distance away I cried,
"O Lord, come and stop these people. Stop them, Lord,
they are falling into hell." He looked at me sadly, and
said, "You stop them." I told Him I had tried and
failed, and that I could not make them hear. Then
He came to me and wrapped me in His Spirit, round
and round, over and underneath, inside and out. He
put me down again and said, "You stop them." I
cried out again, "Stop! Stop!" and some of them
stopped.

After that day in the pasture, I knew that the world was lost, and that it was not enough for me to pray for myself, my people and my friends. I knew that God expected me to stop the multitudes. Indeed, how easy it is for us to run shoulder to shoulder with lost humanity and not either see or hear the passing multitudes.

MY FIRST ATTEMPT TO SUPPORT THE CHURCH PROGRAM

Our church had a debt. Our people were very poor. On Sunday morning they were to raise money to cover the interest and a small payment on the principal of the debt. While in prayer, the Lord asked me if I didn't think we could raise the entire debt of twenty-seven dollars, if we tried hard. I was sure it could be done, and felt that I could pledge a dollar, although I did not have any money and did not know where I could get any. Money was very scarce in those days. After making this decision, I was very happy, and full of faith for the whole amount. Then the Lord gave me a little message, and told me I was to stand up on Sunday morning and speak to the people, and raise the offering. I was trembling with fear and was full of excuses. As the time drew near, I was sure God had spoken to me, and that I would have to obey or I would displease Him. I tried to work among the Christians, and even approached two members of the church board, hoping all the time that some of them would get stirred, and find an easier way to get the money. But they said I was young and inexperienced, and did not understand their battles with poverty. I hoped I would get sick so I could not go to church, but Sunday morning found me perfectly well and thoroughly frightened. I could not see why God could not find a better way than to ask me to do such a terrifying task. I waited just as long as I could, and then got up and tried to tell the people what God had told me. I was so frightened that I broke down and wept. In three minutes I had twenty-six dollars in silver, and my own one dollar pledge which was not yet paid.

After church, when I remembered that I would have to find a dollar before eleven o'clock Monday morning, I felt distressed, and intended to go to the pasture to pray about the matter, but the pastor asked me to go to the little schoolhouse where I had been saved to lead the afternoon testimony meeting. I took some of the younger girls, and we walked the eight miles between services. God blessed us, and we thought it was one of the best meetings we had ever attended. When I was saying good-by to the people, old Brother Gray left a big silver dollar in my hand, as he thanked me for coming to help them while their pastor was ill. I forgot to say, "Thank you," so eager was I to run back to View to give my dollar to the man who had the other twenty-six dollars in hand. This was the first time I ever made a pledge, the first time I ever took an offering, and the first time God ever gave me money.

After a time I attended my first missionary meeting in an assembly at Portland, Oregon, having been sent up there as a delegate from our little church. The appeal was for money to rebuild a hut in Swaziland which had been burned. I had twenty dollars, and felt that if I would give that, others would add enough to finish that building, but I was afraid to stand up among strange people to make the pledge, and I hesitated until it was too late. I had the bill in my hand. A few minutes later some men sitting behind me left the meeting. I thought I might as well put the bill back in my purse. But when I looked, it was gone. I promised God that if He would help me get the bill again, He should surely have it all. But I never saw the twenty dollars again, and Miss Innis did not get her new hut in Africa.

COLLEGE EXPERIENCES

All my life I had wanted to be a teacher. I had pushed on in school, even though I had to work for room, board and books. Now when I was about ready to begin my life's work, I felt that God wanted me to go to college and prepare to work for Him. I loved my home, my people and my friends, and was satisfied with the plans I had made for my life, but always I was confronted with these words, "Lovest thou me more than these?" I was not sure whether I loved Him more, but I sincerely wanted to do so, and He conquered again. I had enough money to buy two tickets to Nampa, Idaho. So I took my sister Florence, who had

lately been converted, and persuaded the two Bevard
girls that they too needed to go to Bible school.
We reached Nampa in the night. Having no friends,
and no money with which to go to the hotel, we stayed
in the cold station until morning. During this time
we had our first introduction to an irrigation ditch. In
the moonlight it looked like cement, so we stepped in.

Brother Harry Hayes had held a meeting at View,
so when we saw his name in the telephone directory,
we decided to call him. He came to the station and
took us to his home for breakfast and a little rest. I
learned that day that the Hayes family needed a boy
to milk their cow, and do the outside work. I needed
a place to live, and could do that boy's work, so I got
the job. To pay my tuition I taught a few subjects,
and acted as substitute teacher.

During my college years I had many unusual experiences as a fill-in. If the primary teacher did not
come, I took her place. If the cook was ill, I prepared
the meals. Sometimes it was the waiter or the scrub-
woman whose work fell to me. When necessary I
taught the Bible classes for Professor Marshall, and
the Theory of Medicine for Dr. Mangum. When someone was ill, I tried to be a nurse; when a pastor was
unable to get to his appointment, I acted as supply.
One time the evangelist was unable to keep her appointment, so they sent me to see if I could help out.
All the way up to Halfway, where the meeting was to
be held, the train wheels seemed to mock me, saying,
"What are you going to preach? What are you going

to preach?" I was matron of the girls' dormitory one year. One year I was manager of the club—the dining hall. Dr. Wiley once said he was going away for a day and leave me as president, so I could say I had been everything from bootblack to college president. I did not understand it then, but when I got to Africa I saw why God led me in those very paths.

I always had to fight poverty. I wore the same scotch-plaid dress for years. Pencils and postage stamps became subjects of prayer. One time, in my junior year of college, I decided I would have to leave school for a season to get money for clothes and books. I went home from school early so I would have time to tell God all about my decision before I started to prepare the evening meal. As soon as I got on my knees, the Lord said to me, "What is it you need?" I quickly named off books, tuition and a dozen articles of clothing. As I talked with the Lord I found I could not truthfully say I needed any single thing that very afternoon, so I went back to school ashamed of my hastiness.

Soon after this I really did need many things, and went home early to have a talk with God. This time He did not come so soon, but at midnight He came to the kitchen where I was studying my Greek lesson, He told me He had heard me calling, and asked what I needed. I began to tell Him how He had sent me to college, but that my way had been a very hard way. Others had what they needed. Some had parents who could help them. Some had friends who paid their bills. But it seemed to me that I was about the only one who had no money at all for the things for which students need money. He stretched out His hands. They were covered with gold. He said I could have my choice. I could take the money I needed or He would arrange for somebody to pay my bills or I could leave it with Him as it had been before. He assured me that He had sent me to school, that He wanted to be the one to help me, to pay my bills and to see me through. When I realized that He had been looking after me all the time while I was so fearful and slow of heart, I was very much ashamed and could not look at Him. When I at last found courage to look up, He was gone. For days my heart burned with a new sense of His presence, and from then on I learned to trust Him for my needs. Time and again He got to me—sometimes at the last minute, but always in time.

One time He told me to pledge five hundred dollars in a money raising campaign for the college. This was a great test for my faith. I had saved a few dollars to buy a graduation dress, but He asked me for this money. I received a small check for some work I had done. He asked me for that check. My obligations were so many, and my money so insufficient that I didn't think it mattered much anyway. I gladly gave it all to Him, and in less than half an hour thereafter, God sent Brother Emerson to the office to pay all my account there. Friends presented me with a whole graduation outfit, so I had sixty-five dollars for the offering, the clothes I needed, and a receipt for my college expenses.

On Sunday morning I gave my sixty-five dollars, but received no blessing. I noticed that Dr. Winchester was not at the service, and I wished she had asked me to write her name on the blackboard for at least five hundred dollars. I opened my Bible, and these words seemed to jump out of the page and stand up before me: "Put that on my account" (Philemon 18). Why was it harder for me to trust God for five hundred dollars than to trust Dr. Winchester? I wanted to be ready for Africa, and I did not want to be presumptuous, so I tarried. That night the meeting was about to close, and they were yet a few thousand dollars from their goal. In desperation I asked God to speak to me again. I opened my Bible and read, "I pray thee give pledges, and I will deliver thee two thousand horses, if thou be able on thy part to set riders upon them" (II Kings 18: 23). That was enough. With desperate effort, I pulled myself from the seat, and wrote on the little blackboard, "Pledge $500, paid $65." When the people saw the amount I had written, they began again to pledge, and amidst much demonstration, they ran the amount several thousand dollars beyond the goal of $25,000. Out in Africa when I needed large sums of money to carry on the work of God, I understood the lessons He had given me in finances while at Northwest Nazarene College.

Also while in college I learned how to prevail with God. I learned how to win souls. I learned how to pray down revivals. One time a small group of students prayed seven nights in succession. In the morning after that last night, God came mightily upon us. The chapel service started in the morning and ran all day. Classes were dismissed, and a great revival came upon the whole school and church. Students wept and exhorted, and great conviction fell upon the unsaved. We prayed all night in the dormitories, and in the homes of the people. Dozens found God, and many were sanctified wholly. There was extemporaneous preaching in the classrooms, in the chapel, in the regular services of the church, and sometimes the altar was opened the second and even the third time in one service. Years afterward, out in Africa, in the face of terrible odds, in this very way, we prayed down revivals, and pushed through to glorious victory. I was able to stand alone, when necessary, and battle through seeming impossibilities, because I had been along that way before and knew that revivals come from God, and that He will answer prayer, if we wait for Him.

One time, out in Africa, we had a wonderful service. Everybody came to the altar, but before there was any victory, Satan seemed to take complete control of everything. The seeking heathen stretched out on the grass and went to sleep. Some demon-possessed persons began to foam at the mouth and make roaring sounds like animals. The heavens turned to brass. I walked up and down in desperation, looking at these people. I could not pray. I longed for someone to help. Then I remembered that Jesus died for these very men and women, and that He was able to save and change them, and that not even the powers of hell could keep victory from these seekers, if we would only wait until God came. I knew from experience that if we waited for God, He would surely come. I knew the people would not go away without my permission, so I told the devil he might as well move on, for we were going to wait until God came. I told the devil he was already defeated, for I could sit there longer than he could, and that in the end God would come. I walked around the seekers and claimed them every one for the Lord. I began to praise the Lord, and told Him He would find us there when He came. In a few minutes everyone was on his knees praying loudly, and soon some began to find victory. As the sun came up in the morning, the last girl had just made peace with God, and everyone was happy and rejoicing in his new found love.

I settled my call to Africa, and received the gift of the Holy Ghost during my college days. I had experienced a wonderful conversion, and for a time did not feel need of any further work of grace in my heart. I tried to accept this great gift of the Holy Spirit, but always felt unsatisfied. I often wondered if there is any such great cleansing as that which we heard preached. I often went to the altar to pray for seekers, when in reality I was praying for myself.

Three things troubled me: I still wanted to follow the
plans I had made for my life; I was afraid God wanted
me to preach; and was afraid that God was going to
send me to Africa as a missionary. If I had been sure
God was calling me, I would have cast aside my plans.
I didn't like to see or hear women preach. I thought
it was dangerous enough for a man to be a holiness
preacher, to say nothing of a woman. I thought it
would be certain starvation. But worst of all was
Africa. I had but little conception of what it means
to be a missionary. I did not know how anyone should
go about it to get to the field. Once, when a child, I had
seen in a farm paper a picture of cannibals preparing
to cook the missionary in a big black pot. I thought
one would be in constant danger of becoming food for
a cannibal feast. But above all this, I was not sure God
was calling me, so I was confused, and thought I
might be deceived.

One morning on my way to school, down by the
irrigation ditch, I came into the midst of a very large
flock of restless, bleating sheep. When I got right into
the center of the flock, I forgot they were sheep, and
thought I was hearing the cries of the heathen—dying
without God. It seemed that the Lord lifted me up, and
put me on a balcony high above the earth. He told me
to look toward the east. I saw all the lands of the
Yellow Race, where people thronged the streets, rowed
up and down the rivers and ran through the fields. As
I looked very closely at these multiplied millions of
little people, I saw that every one of them had four

hands, four eyes, and two mouths. With two eyes they looked at their work or play, as all other men do; with the other two eyes they gazed up toward heaven. With two hands they held the plow or basket, and worked as other men do; but the other two hands were stretched up toward God. One mouth laughed or cursed or spoke words of wisdom; but the other mouth cried loudly to God for mercy and peace until the heavens rang with the pitiful wails of the millions without God. Now the bleating of the sheep were the cries of the multitudes of yellow people who were dying while waiting and longing for a Saviour.

The Lord told me to look to the south. Here I saw the brown men and women of India in the Ganges River and in the temples. I saw the masses thronging up and down the streets and lanes like lost sheep driven by the storm and without guide or shepherd. Here again I saw what I had seen in other lands.

Then I looked toward Latin America with her needy millions. I could see the two hands lifted to God, the two longing eyes pleading for rest, and could hear the cries from the lips of those who sought for God all up and down those broad lands to the south.

Then He turned me about and we looked toward the great continent of Africa. A great black cloud covered the whole land. A terrible storm was on. Peals of thunder shook the heavens. The lightning flashed, and I saw the land carpeted with bleached, white bones—bones of the generations of men who have lived and died and gone into eternity without ever once hearing the name of Jesus. Another flash, and on top of the carpet of bones I saw a layer of the corpses of men and women who had just died—those who had lived in this generation, but had now gone to where no message of hope could ever reach them. Again the lightning flamed, and on top of these dead forms, huddled together in terrible fear, were more than one hundred and fifty million black people who today stagger on in the dark without the light of Christ to guide them. Every frightened and protruding eye looked wildly up to God. Every hand reached out in a desperate effort to grasp something to save them from the fury of the storm, and now the bleating of the sheep were the cries of these millions of lost people in Africa.

Then He showed me our own fair land. I saw people in every walk of life. Even my friends and neighbors were there. This caused me to marvel more than anything I had seen before: the fact that white men, just like yellow, brown and black men had each four eyes, four arms and two mouths, and the fact that they all looked and reached up and cried to God. I saw the beautifully dressed women on the dance floor, the drunk in the gutter, the moral man that I had known and who I thought had no desire for God. These, together with the neighbor that lived next door to me, were all looking up with longing eyes, reaching out with grasping fingers trying to get hold of something that would sustain them, and every mouth was calling, ever calling, for that rest that only God can give. Now the bleating of the sheep were the cries of my people, my friends and my countrymen.

With broken heart I tried to explain to the Christ who had shed His blood that all the world might be saved, how I had not realized that all men, no matter how they acted, were hungry and were crying to Him for soul rest. He looked at me with a sad, tired face, when I asked if He could not go away and rest awhile. I asked Him if He must always, night and day, listen to these pitiful cries. He answered in a sad voice, "Child, I never rest." I fell at His feet weeping, and asked Him to tell me how I could help. Again I looked, and here and there upon the earth were people praying. I saw a man on a hilltop, a woman in a secret closet, and others shut away in secret places groaning under the burden of prayer. Then I felt the heavens shaken, and saw the arm of God begin to move. Channels were opened, and men were set free from their horrible chains of darkness.

After this experience I could not rest. I was hungry and dissatisfied, and was always hearing the cries of the heathen. One noon hour, after weeks of wrestling with God, I went into a classroom and locked the door. I told the Lord I had come to settle my call, and that I did not intend to go out that door until it was forever settled. I began with my life's plans. I promised God I would work no more on them unless I had direct orders from the Almighty to do so. Preach? I would try. I decided that it would be no more painful to starve to death as a despised woman preacher than to perish of famine in my soul. I was so hungry after more of God that life itself meant little to me, if I could not be satisfied.

Then Africa loomed up. It was not enough to preach in America—I must preach in Africa. I remembered the cannibal's pot. I saw myself away out in the jungle. I was dressed in a hideous black dress that began at my ankles and reached to my fingers and my ears. My hair was pulled back straight, and pinned in a little tight knob on the top of my head. Since there are no doctors in a land of cannibals, all my teeth except two or three were gone. I sat on an old soap box by the side of a grass hut while a few naked children played at my feet. I started up in fear, and then I heard myself saying right out loud, "Lord God Almighty, you have a little old woman on your hands from this very moment, now, and throughout eternity."

I had scarcely finished the sentence when something like a great iron weight slipped off me, and went splashing down into space beneath. I jumped to my feet, feeling as light as a feather. The room seemed to be on fire with the presence of God. Fear and hunger had gone, and I was free and satisfied. My heart was aflame with the love of God. I loved His will for me. I felt willing, and wanted to start immediately for Africa. I had not only settled my call, but had been baptized with the Holy Ghost.

So wonderful was the work done in my heart that day that not once through the years has it ever been

suggested that God did not call me and send me across
the sea. Not once did I ever doubt that God did really
baptize me with His Spirit, and completely cleanse
and satisfy my soul. Many, many times in Swaziland
I defeated discouragement and failure by remembering that the great God of heaven sent me there to
represent Him, and that He would make me succeed.
Often when I looked at men sunken into the deepest
depths of sin and demon possession, I encouraged myself in the Lord, because I knew that God changed me,
and it is nothing with Him whether they be little or
great sinners.

I cannot express in words what it meant to me to
have those years in a holiness college. How grateful
we ought to be to the Lord for our wonderful colleges
where young men and young women may learn Christian soldiery before they are thrust out into the front
ranks of the battle line.

Appointment as a Missionary

One Sunday morning, late in 1919, the First Church
of the Nazarene at Nampa, Idaho, was told that I was
to be recommended for appointment as a missionary
to Africa at the January Board Meeting in Kansas
City. In a few minutes over fifty people promised to
pay one dollar each month for a period of five years to
provide my salary for that time. Friends on the
Idaho-Oregon District supplied money for passage and
other expenses. One night I came home to find my
room full of all kinds of beautiful gifts, some of them

very expensive gifts, including practically everything I would need for my equipment. Then they sent me to Kansas City to meet the Missionary Board, and I was appointed to go that year as soon as they could secure passports and permits.

When at last I said good-by to my friends and loved ones, I felt as though long ago I had walked into the big end of a long tunnel, and now must go straight on through, although I had now come to the little end where the opening was so very narrow that it pinched and bruised both my body and my heart.

I knew but little about traveling, but I started out alone on the day coach with a big box of lunch, two heavy cases, my typewriter, a heavy coat and other small parcels as hand luggage. I didn't know a red cap when I met him, and had never ridden in a taxi, so when no one met me at the station in New York City, I took my many pieces of luggage and tried to make my way on the underground railway to the one address that had been given me. The journey took me completely across the city, and I was very tired after my sleepless nights on the train while coming across the continent. I felt like a lost rat, and wondered how man could possibly dig so many tunnels under the earth. The Lord saw me there, and sent kind people to help His bewildered child.

First Impressions in Africa

It was Thanksgiving Day. The little Sabie train was racing along at its usual rate of ten miles per hour. At noon time I was hungry and a bit lonesome. I could but remember that at home they were eating dinner together, and that I was alone in a very strange land—and hungry.

We stopped at a little station, and the people all ran out to a grass shed. I followed, and got a cup of tea which was as black as coffee, and half a cooky. This was my Thanksgiving dinner, and my introduction to South African tea. I comforted myself with the thought that in the evening my long journey would be over, we would arrive at the mission station, and Mrs. Shirley would have a big Thanksgiving dinner waiting for us. When we arrived at the Shirley home I was astonished that Mrs. Shirley said nothing about the holiday. She had been away from the States so long that she had forgotten it was Thanksgiving Day. I understood this in later years.

In the evening the church building was filled with natives who wanted to see their new missionaries. As I looked in amazement upon these people, I wondered if I would ever be of any use in that land; for they all looked alike to me. I could not tell the difference between men and women or between boys and girls. The building looked to me like a huge box of chocolates, and the only difference between the drops was that some were bigger than others.

The mission station was still in the process of building. The sand was full of fleas. The visiting missionary who slept in the same room with me that

night got up to catch fleas that were troubling her
sleeping children. She bagged sixty-seven in the
one catch, but I did not even enter the chase; I was
too far gone, and knew it would be of no avail. I had
worried about being eaten by cannibals. Now I saw
there was not the remotest danger of such an end, but
I knew there was imminent danger of being eaten
alive by the sand fleas.

First Duties

The very first morning I began to study the Zulu
language. Mrs. Shirley always conducted the Sunday
morning service. She said I was to get up every week
before she began to preach and say everything I could
say in Zulu. She said it might not do the natives much
good, but it would be wonderfully good for me, and
it was. Every Sunday morning I tried to testify or
exhort. During the week I went out to visit the near-
by neighbors. They would sit down in the shade of
their grass huts and help me with my vocabulary. I
could smile, when I could not talk; so I made friends.
My first convert was the wife of a witch doctor—one
of the women who did so much to help me with the
language. One day when all the missionaries were
away from the station, I tried to preach my first sermon in Zulu, and this woman came to the altar and
was wonderfully converted.

I was given the medical and educational work. My
drug store was a soap box. Dr. Mangum once said to
his class that one could be quite a good doctor and use

only five or six drugs. I had that many—sulphur for itch; quinine, aspirin and epsom salts for malaria; iodine, boracic acid powder and permanganate for disinfectants; a pair of forceps for toothache and—that was about all. I always was afraid I would kill somebody or let someone die needlessly. But many were cured in those days, mainly by means of desperate prayer.

My day school was composed of a few dozen children ranging in age from infants to full grown boys and girls. I first tried to arrange them on benches, but soon found out this would be about as difficult as teaching them to read. Every time I looked there were more bright eyes and little squirming forms under the seats than on them. So I moved the benches out and sat my pupils on the floor. They all yelled to the tops of their voices as they studied. When I asked why, they said, "This is the way it is done in this country. Everybody does it this way. How would you know who was and who was not studying, if they did not study aloud?"

I taught in the night school too. Men from the gold mines wanted to learn to read, so they came every weeknight to study reading, spelling and figures for a couple of hours. We taught them to read the Bible and to write their names, and then we read the Scriptures and prayed with them. We won many converts in the compounds by these methods. I spent four years at my first station, Sabie, in the Transvaal.

SWAZILAND: MY FIRST VISIT THERE

Most of our Nazarene work in Africa was in Swaziland, and I was very anxious to see this field and our workers there. At the first quarterly meeting time I went to Barberton, Transvaal, on the train. Mr. Penn met me there with the horses. The new missionaries for Swaziland would usually come to this town, and ride on horseback over the mountains, while their trunks and boxes would follow—often after many months—on a longer route by donkey or ox teams.

It was a very rainy day when I reached Barberton. Early in the morning we began to climb the Barberton Mountain. Higher and higher we went over rolling stones and narrow ledges. As soon as we reached the top, we started down the other side, and the saddle which was not too new or strong continually threatened to slip over the horse's head. When down that side, we forded a fast rising river, hurried across a little valley, and started up another range of hills. We climbed "The Devil's Stairway"—a rocky climb over larger rocks—and on up into the third range where at the top we came to the approach of "The Devil's Bridge." We crept along the little path that wound around the edge of the mountain, and listened to the howling of the wind in the valley beneath and to the left of us. It sounded worse than it was. The narrow natural bridge, but a few feet in width, had a deep canyon on either side. Once across, we galloped our horses whenever we found a few feet of level ground, and so we arrived at Camp—the common missionary designation of our Piggs Peak Station—before dark. I did not mind the long day's ride in the storm, for I was reared in the West, and had ridden horses since I was a child. It was a different matter with people reared in the city, who had never ridden on horseback, and for parents with young children who were afraid of horses and of natives.

SWAZILAND: MY HOME FOR SIXTEEN YEARS

Swaziland has been called, "The Switzerland of Africa," because of its many beautiful and rugged mountain peaks. It was here at the old Peniel (original native name Endingeni) Station, now rechristened Schmelzenbach Memorial Station, that Rev. Harmon Schmelzenbach began our first Nazarene work in Africa. I was assigned there, as matron of the Girls' Home, in 1924. For four years I had the wonderful privilege of working with Harmon Schmelzenbach, the great missionary, and from him learned many very valuable lessons. I was given charge of the day school, and helped with the district work. When Brother Schmelzenbach died I was given charge of the station and the surrounding district.

In the Girls' Home we cared for hundreds of girls and young women who sought a home with us because of heathen marriage customs that were incompatible with Christianity. Words can never tell what those young women meant to me. We were knitted together by tribulation and distress, by persecutions and famines, by nakedness, peril and sword. Through all God made us more than conquerors, and we found in Jesus Christ unsearchable riches of grace, wisdom, life, power and all blessings.

I always had a troop of orphan children about me. From the wee witch babies in the soap boxes to the chirping urchins who sometimes serenaded me at my bedroom window before sunup—I love them every one. I hope that God will find in them some rare jewels for His kingdom. During the last years, our entire family numbered over two hundred souls.

I was reared on the farm. I love farming. So it was not an unpleasant task to care for a big station and supervise a farm of over two hundred acres. The family raised almost all our own food, for we could not afford to hire help or buy corn, beans, pumpkins, sweet potatoes and fruit. These we produced on our land. We worked hard, and had many a good time racing down a long row planting, hoeing or husking corn. We kept our home aglow with brilliant colored flowers and trees — beautiful jacarandas, flaming poinsettias, purple bougainvilleas and begonias of every sort. We pruned orchards, repaired engines and machinery, planted trees, cared for stock and did all the other work that goes along with regular farming.

I learned a lot about building. Many times I shoveled dirt, dug sand, plastered mud walls, helped make bricks, and mixed cement to encourage the native people while we were building our schools and chapels.

I rode thousands of miles on my old red mule,
Coffee, over hills and velds supervising the Bush
schools and holding church meetings and revivals. I
loved this work very much. I learned dearly to love
the night skies with their shining Southern Cross
over the bushveld. I lived in the kraals of the people,
ate their food, slept many a night on the floor with my
saddle for a pillow, forded the rivers at midnight, got
caught in terrible storms, walked in the burning sands,
and in later years got stuck in rivers or in the mud with
my Chevrolet. But I loved it all. I loved the old
people and never tired of hearing about their troubles.
I loved the young people, and delighted to help them
solve their problems. I was never happier than when
I galloped along with an army of bright-eyed little
boys and girls who were screeching and racing me to
yonder big stone.

Before Miss Chism came, I was principal of the
Main Station School. Afterward I took part in teaching classes in agriculture, native study, housewifery,
sewing, etc.

For many years when we could not have a white
nurse of our own, I supervised the medical work,
nursed the sick, pulled teeth by the hundreds, set
misplaced joints, delivered babies, etc. God blessed
me in a very unusual way in this work. I knew my
limitations, and I always called on the Great Physician, and in the hardest places I mostly depended on
prayer. Some years we would care for as many as 250

inpatients, and give as many as six or seven thousand outpatient treatments.

I must not forget to tell you of the multiplied hours I spent in *izindaba* (listening to appeals and passing judgments). Many a night the missionary sits all night—until the sun comes up in the morning —trying to hear and remember all that is said, so he will be prepared to pass righteous judgments. This is very important work, but very nerve-racking and heartrending.

During my spare time I wrote hundreds of letters to America, kept station and district books, etc. My missionary labors were many and varied. I labored for the people—from the cradle to the grave I was with them. At birth I was present to serve, in sickness I nursed them, in health I taught them, I performed the marriages for the young people, I buried the dead —even making coffins and digging graves for some.

Of course I went to Africa primarily to preach the gospel, and this I tried to do amidst all other activities, and above all other duties. I tried to study and pray and be prepared to preach in season and out of season. I held dozens of revivals every year, and saw many souls find Christ. God was good to me and gave me rich rewards in jewels for His crown.

When I went to Africa our Nazarene work was in its beginnings. I saw it grow and progress far toward a self-supporting, self-governing and self-propagating church. Surely God was good to me, and good to His

missionaries and native Christians in our Nazarene
field in Africa.

Miss Irene Jester was my associate on the field
for a number of years, and is at this writing still there
and doing a fine work. Once when I was preparing
a report for the annual Council meeting, she wrote a
poem "With Apologies to Kipling," especially for me.
The lines are so fitting in describing the missionary
life that I append them here:

IF

If you can rise before the day is dawning
    And pray for grace and strength and wisdom, too,
And be prepared, with each new-coming morning
    To hear the sound from front and back door, too,
Of boys and girls and men and women calling
    For nails or tools or soap or work or clothes,
Or yet perhaps to hear an old man bawling,
    "Could you take out this tooth do you suppose?"

If you can skimp to try to save each shilling
    And yet hold nothing as your very own,
But with each new request be gladly willing
    To give your choicest treasures as a loan;
If you can give instructions to a native
    A dozen times or more as like as not
And then be patient with his words so plaintive
    "Hau, mina, ngi kohliwe—(I forgot)."

If you can act as doctor, nurse, or teacher,
  And lawyer, farmer, builder all combined
And be foremost a faithful gospel preacher
  And ne'er grow weary, thoughtless, or unkind;
If you can take a load like this to carry
  And leave each failure and success with Jesus, too,
You're sure to be a first-class missionary
  And know the joys that missionaries do.

Good-by: I'd Do It Again

I never like to say good-by. It was hard to leave all the loved places and things of Endingeni Station on which I had bestowed so many years of arduous labor. I knew I might be riding my mule, Coffee, for the last time over the hills, valleys and velds of the Piggs' Peak District in beautiful Swaziland. Africa had become my home. America seemed foreign to me. But the wonderful people with whom I had been living and working for almost an unbroken twenty years were the cause of my real distress when I came to say good-by. The missionaries with whom I had such wonderful fellowship seemed almost like my own brothers and sisters. The national workers, the native Christians, and even the heathen friends seemed like my very own children.

Hundreds of natives came in to mourn my leaving, and most of them left a little piece of money with which "to buy food by the way." They are so often hungry in their journeys that they feared I would be thin by the time I reached America. They said they wanted me to be plump and beautiful, so my people would see that I came from friends who loved and appreciated me. The majority of these gifts were tickies and six-pences (nickels and dimes), but when I counted them all, I had $125.00. Since I did not need much food for the way, when I arrived in the United States I bought a lovely portable Corona typewriter, and a suitcase with my bread money.

One of the old heathen chiefs said, "The whole world is rotten since I heard that you are going away. We are all now naked. There will never come another man who will so love and care for me and for my people." But when he heard that Fairy Chism was to take my place, he was comforted, for he likes her very much. One man wrote and said, "Good-by, Dulile [my native name]. You are a man. Your words are man's words. Your judgments are man's judgments. Your works are man's works." A spokesman for another neighborhood said, "You are a man, Dulile, a real man. You are a man with a long, long beard [he showed with his hands how long the beard]. From today we shall be orphans. We shall be just like a family of little children whose father is dead." In Africa one needs only to be a man, especially a man with a long beard, to be the greatest of God's creation.

The national workers gave me as a parting gift a warrior's costume. One preacher dressed in the leopard skins and cow tails, with battle axe and spears. And before the gathered assembly another preacher

presented the gift and told me its meaning. In the
days before the white man came, once the warrior
donned these battle garments, he never took them off
until the victory was won. It was perfectly honorable
to die fully clad in battle, but it was absolutely un-
pardonable for a true warrior to remove his garments
except as a victor. As they gave me the present, they
promised they would never lay down their burden
as leaders except in death or victory at the coming
of the Lord.

If I had my life to live again, and if God would
grant me the great privilege, I would gladly make
every preparation and go again to Africa. I would
joyfully accept any burden, and pour out my all for
her worthy, lovable people. I know of no place in all
the world where one can better serve God and humanity than in the great needy continent of Africa.

PART TWO—PEN PICTURES

1. *Nuggets of Black Gold*

a) Lighthouses.

Once I asked an old witch doctor, "What do you think of the preacher we put here to live in your neighborhood? Is he a Christian? Have you seen anything in his life or his home?" The old man was walking by the side of my mule. He was arrayed in skins, cow tails, teeth, pouches and horns containing his medicines. He looked up at me, his smile gone, and said, "Child of God! That man!" He lifted his hand and pointed to the little grass and mud home of our preacher: a home that was brighter, larger, more sanitary and convenient than the homes of the heathen. A few fruit and shade trees could be seen growing inside a pretty hedge; and everything was clean and in order round about. The old man stopped, his bony finger still pointing to the preacher's little home, sparkling before us in the freshness and beauty of a sunny African morning, and said, "Daughter of the King, that is our lamp. That is the light of the Swazi nation."

In these days, more than ever, much depends upon our native workers. They are the most important part of the native church. The worker, his words, his actions, his life, his home, his wife, and his children are being watched day and night by scores of clever heathen, as well as by his Christian flock.

b) Old Solomon.

Old Solomon, our first evangelist in Africa, and a mighty soul winner, says he will not be keeper of God's vineyard, and, like Solomon of old, neglect his own vineyard. His greatest revival was what he called "Solomon's revival." When the unsaved did not seek Christ, he said the reason might be in the leader. He announced his revival and insisted that all the people be present. On Sunday morning he stood up before his church and confessed his own failures and the failures of his flock. He quoted many promises for strength and for victory for the people of God, and then went to the altar himself. He gathered all his church about him, and insisted that everyone pray long and loudly for Solomon, the pastor. This praying stopped only when Solomon was blessed. God poured out His blessing, and, as Solomon said, "sharpened his armor." After this he had a revival for the church. Solomon's church is alive. It grows rapidly. Heathen are always at their services. His Sunday school and his day school are the largest in any of our outstations. His people are good livers, good prayers, and diligent seekers of the lost.

Solomon came up to Endingeni to see me one Monday morning. His face was aglow. His poor dim eyes were shining with new light. He told me that he had walked so far with God that he was now closer to heaven than to earth, that he had looked heavenward so long that the light of the city had blinded his eyes until he could no longer plainly see the things of earth, that he had listened so long to the beautiful music from above that it had drowned out the sounds of this earth. The day before, he said, he had felt that his time was very, very short, and he wished to do much for the Master. He felt that he could not be satisfied unless God helped him to win ten souls on his Monday's trip, so he arose shortly after midnight and prayed. When the first rooster crowed he saddled his little donkey and started. He had come seventeen miles, and had stopped at every kraal in the way, and had earnestly and passionately begged the people to seek Christ. He had won seven souls that morning, and was confident he would find the other three before the sun went down. Solomon is one of the biggest nuggets we ever found.

c) Vabaye.

Vabaye's sister was given to the old chief for ten head of cattle. As a special favor Vabaye was thrown in for the token payment of four or five head (a very common practice when more than one girl is taken by one man from the same family). Now the chief was fat and old, and was the husband of many wives. Vabaye was young and independent, and loved life and youth. Without knowing it was her wedding day, she carried the big clay pot full of beer to the home of her sister. There she saw that if she ever escaped, she would have to act quickly. While the other girls were bathing at sundown in the near-by stream,

Vabaye sneaked off in the tall grass and began to run for her life. As the terrible African darkness settled about her, she heard that she was being followed by men and dogs. When she could run no more, she hid in a pile of stones, and could not be found—for God hid her.

When she reached home the next day, and found that she would surely be dragged away to this heathen man, if she longer stayed, she wrapped her few belongings in a little rag, and started for the Transvaal. On the way she heard the missionary teaching his class about Jesus. Hidden there in the grass, Vabaye thought about the missionary's God. To herself, she said, "They say He is a hiding place. Perhaps I can hide in Him." She made her way to where Brother Schmelzenbach was, and gave her heart to God.

For many years Vabaye was almost a prisoner. She was an outcast, and could not visit her home. Her angry brother made it unsafe for her to leave the mission station. She learned to pray, and was a great blessing in the work. At her baptism she took the name Alice. For seventeen years she has cooked for the single women missionaries on the Schmelzenbach Memorial Station. All the white people in northern Swaziland know Alice for her wonderful cooking. No southern mammy could be more zealous and faithful for her children than is Alice of Swaziland for her missionaries. God bless her dear heart! She is a consistent, all round Christian. She won both her old parents for the Lord. In 1940, after waiting seventeen long years for her freedom, Alice, helped by some Tennessee girls, Fairy Chism, Irene Jester and me, got cattle and bought herself from her heathen brother.

Alice is a good, strong preacher. Along with her duties as cook, she has mothered the many children of the station, been chief adviser of the girls in the home, carried a special burden for the old and the sick, helped in revivals, and acted as assistant pastor, without pay, at the Endingeni church. But her greatest talent is her ability to pray and get things from God.

I shall never forget how God spoke to my heart one midnight, as I listened to Alice's praying. That prayer, one of the mightiest prayers I have ever heard, was one of the greatest and sweetest experiences of my life in Africa. I was working on night duty with the sick. In a manner that could not be denied, she was calling one by one the names of the unsaved that lived about in that neighborhood, and was begging God to do everything He could to save them. My heart was tremendously stirred, for I knew God would answer that prayer. I felt as if I had never truly prayed myself.

For weeks that lone intercessor had been spending hours every night in prayer. Sometimes she cried out in a loud voice. At other times, when it was quiet in her room, I saw through the window her cot untouched, and stretched on the grass mat on the floor, her open Bible before a little tallow candle, lay Alice, her eyes swollen from weeping, her words turned into groans as she went down into the valley of suffering, seeking the lost. When I asked her one day if she were not afraid her physical strength would fail from so much loss of sleep, she looked at me with a glow of unearthly light on her face, and said, "Daughter of the King, if you only knew: before me is Christ, behind me it is light. If I reach to the right hand or to the left, I find the strength of God. I will stop when God gives me what I ask." Three months passed. One morning at daybreak, a heathen man came and called Alice, telling her that for three months God had been dealing with his soul night and day. On the cement steps before the mission home, he gave his heart to God. The revival began, and in a special meeting that ended in an effort to reach the unsaved, and as a result of that meeting, scores of heathen were born into the kingdom of God. The climax came one morning when Gideon preached from Numbers 21: 8, 9, "When he looked, he lived." God came upon that great, dark-skinned congregation as they squatted on the grass covering of the cement floor of the big tabernacle, and twenty-two sought God for the first time in their lives, and found Him. Alice prayed, and the neighborhood was shaken. Vabaye's worth is above that of all the gold in Johannesburg.

d) Glimpses of Lillian.

A big revival was in progress: everywhere people were praying. Lillian was curled up in a ball, lying on the floor. She had lain there almost motionless for hours. She had not tasted food in several days. Someone came to tell me that Lillian was dying. I went to her, and could see by the look on her face that she was praying. She was dying to the world. Slowly and deliberately, she got the last thing settled, and God did a work in her heart that made her a shining light from that day to this.

I remember a certain Sunday service. Lillian stood barefoot in the center of a little mud church. Every inch of the floor was covered with earnest, hungry listeners. The holes in the walls that were made for windows were filled with black faces. God was anointing His handmaiden. She looked like a being from another world. Her face absolutely beamed with the glory of God. A young heathen girl stood up, lifted her hand, and said, "I choose the Lord." Another repeated those sweet words. There was a hushed stillness over our hearts. We felt as if Jesus himself had come into our midst.

At another time we were in an all night meeting. Seekers had been at the altar for a long time. It was hard to pray. Nobody was getting victory. We all felt defeated and sleepy. Suddenly Lillian jumped to her feet, grabbed the first seeker within her reach, shook her soundly and called into her ear, "Pray!" she went down the altar shaking one after another, praying at the top of her voice, as great tears rolled down her cheeks. In a few minutes sleep had vanished, every one prayed through, and all were filled with joy and victory.

We had a girl who was crippled and distorted in body and mind, and possessed by evil spirits. She would sometimes have five or six terrible spells in one day. During these spells, she would roll on the floor roaring and moaning. It was a great grief to us all. She had no home where she could live. One night as I was talking to God about this girl, she began to scream in a wild and terrible voice. I took Alice and Lillian, and some others of the girls who knew how to pray. We surrounded the unfortunate girl and began to pray. The girl backed into a corner, and stood screaming, as if she would kill anyone who dared approach her. We stood praying, and begging God to help us. The Spirit of the Lord came upon Lillian. She took a step forward, looked the screaming girl in the eye, and prayed loudly. Then she began to shake her dress, and cry, "Shoo! Shoo!" After a bit the girl fell at Lillian's feet subdued. God had used His handmaiden to help us solve one of the most difficult problems.

God has given us as evangelists, preachers, teachers, Bible women and nurses some two hundred and fifty men and women whose worth, any one of them, cannot be measured by the riches of the whole African continent. When Africa is mentioned many people think of sparkling diamonds of Kimberly and yellow gold of Ophir and the Rand. But to me Africa will always mean sparkling uplifted eyes more beautiful than diamonds, and glowing faces of native people, each possessing a soul more priceless than all the riches of the world. Of all the prospectors who have made huge fortunes in the great Dark Continent, none

have ever picked up bigger nuggets of gold than those
the missionaries of the Church of the Nazarene have
found in their faithful national workers.

2. *Miracles in Ebony.*

a) "I'm Rich."

"I'm rich, friends, I'm rich!" cried a smiling Swazi
woman, as she witnessed in the revival to the saving
power of Jesus' blood. She lifted her arms, swung
herself gracefully around among the crowd of dark-
skinned listeners who sat on the floor. She did not
look rich. She was shoeless and hatless. Her only covering was a single, cheap garment that hung loosely
from her shoulders. Her home was a little grass hut
with a mud floor, her bed a mat on the ground, and her
food was scarce and coarse. She could not read or
write, and yet she said she was rich. Her listeners be-
lieved her testimony, for they smiled and nodded and
said, "*Yebo, Make, yebo*" (Yes, Mother, yes). Everyone knew Magagula. She had been demon-possessed.
Many a night, while her children cried for food, she
had lain in a drunken stupor wrapped around a big
beer pot. She had been quarrelsome and unlovely.
The demons now had fled. She was no longer a slave
to snuff and beer. Her children were learning in
school, and were members of the Sunday school. Her
husband who beat her when she first gave her heart
to the Lord, now respected and loved her. She always
had a little offering for her Lord, and her peanuts and
corn were diligently tithed. Her delight was to tell her

friends how the Lord had come and made all things new. She had found the riches of salvation.

b) He Put No Difference Between Us and Them.

"The work will not be so definite in your converts here," said a man whom I met just a few months after I arrived in Africa. I had been telling him of the wonderful heart experience I obtained when I was sanctified. He said I should not be disappointed, that God had little background on which to work in the ordinary heathen, and that I should not expect to get the same results with the African that might rightly be expected among more enlightened people. I answered nothing, but I knew there was little background in me, for I was not brought up in a religious environment, and yet God sanctified me. I determined that when I was able to speak the language, I was going to find out if God could sanctify a native, just as He sanctified me. I was going to find this out in connection with the very first convert who gave evidence of definite preparation to receive the fullness of the blessing.

Months passed. Little Willie came to my night school in Sabie. He was a lad of ten or eleven years of age, who had never known a father's love. His mother was ill, and unable to care for herself and her three children. So Willie provided for their needs the best he could. One night the mother died. Next morning Willie came to tell me that he and the other children were now alone. God spoke to my heart and told me I should try to fill a mother's place with these children.

I took Willie into my home. He soon gave evidence by
a changed life and a clear testimony that he had been
born from above. After some time, I noticed that
Willie was weak and thin, and that he looked distressed and sick. I finally found out that for months
he had been fasting and praying and trying to get
sanctified. He said his heart was vile and black, and
that he had heard us telling of a heart cleansing that
God would give, and he thought that was what he
needed. I soon found that he was troubled over the
necessity of making restitution. I assured him that
this was a very ordinary procedure for many seeking
souls. I gave him a piece of paper, and told him to
write down all that was bothering him. For several
days he lay in the grass, in the sun, and finally came
back with a very long list of things about which God
had been talking to him. Most of the items referred to
things he had stolen in his efforts to suppy the needs
of his sick mother and the family. He had something
to fix up with almost everyone in Sabie—white and
black. He got thinner and yellower day by day until it
seemed his strength would absolutely fail, but God
helped him to press on until he had cleared everything
away, even with the storekeeper, at whose place of
business he had acted as errand boy, and from whom
he had taken many things. He should have been sanctified then, but he was afraid the darkness would come
back, so he would not step out in faith.

I prayed for hours with Willie, and had the missionaries and native Christians to pray with him.

Whenever a visiting preacher came our way, I begged
him to try to help Willie. But all seemed useless. He
would not believe. I feared for the sanity of his mind.
I, too, began to fast and pray. One Sunday afternoon
God reminded me of what I had determined in my
heart when that man told me that God could not sanctify an African as He had sanctified me. Here was a
soul ready for the promised cleansing. Would I put
God to the test? Hope sprang up in my heart when I
recognized that this was the voice of God. I determined I would not fail to do my part. That evening I
called the natives in for a prayer meeting. I talked
to them of God's unchanging faithfulness. I told them
that God had spoken to me about a certain thing, and
that I had come tonight prepared to wait until God
granted me that request. I asked if there was another
who had a definite request that he wished to put before
God, and if he would wait here before God until the
request was granted. Willie put up his hand. I asked
him if he would wait there until the sun came up in
the morning, if necessary. He said he would. I asked
if he would wait until the sun went down the next
evening. He said he would. Then I asked if he would
wait until the sun came up the morning after that, if
necessary. With much trembling, Willie promised to
wait until God came, and that in the meantime, he
would do all he could to meet the conditions. He knelt
in the middle of the altar, and I at the end. Both of us
had gone too far now to turn back. We began to pray
in earnest. It was not more than three minutes until

I knew God was there to sanctify Willie. I arose to my feet, saying, "Do your best for me, Lord. They said you would not do it. It will make all the difference in the world in the way I shall preach from now on, Lord." Willie was now praying in faith, with his little hands stretched up to God. The work was done. He jumped up, and then sat back on a bench where he lifted his hands and sat for a very long time, quietly laughing. His childish face was aglow with heavenly light. Willie was sanctified, "just like God sanctified me."

For years Willie gave almost every cent he made back to God. He would not even buy clothes to keep himself properly covered. He prayed so earnestly that once when I needed him badly and knocked loudly on his door, he did not hear me; he was so absorbed in his talking with God. He was a great soul winner. Tonight I remember two special cases in which Willie led souls to God. One was the case of a poor little sick woman whom he found and led into the kingdom of God. He visited her often during her sickness, and when she died, he stayed with her people, and buried the woman in a Christian's grave. The other case was little Mgwingi, a boy who fell out of a tree and ripped his stomach open. Willie found this boy in his home with his bowels gushed out, and led him to Jesus. He walked the long weary miles over the hills after school, daily, to visit the little lad. Finally we saw that God must spare the child's life, and so we carried him to the Mission dispensary.

During the time when the other missionaries were on furlough, and I was alone on the station, Willie was almost like my right arm, so greatly did he help me in my many and varied labors. He was an efficient teacher, an unctuous preacher, and had mechanical ability. He helped me keep the engines and machinery in repair. For years he did all our carpentry. He, with his brother, Edward, roofed our big tabernacle at Endingeni, and made all the furniture for our dispensary—cupboards, tables, beds for the children, etc.

Willie was the first African I saw sanctified; but, thank God, he was not the last one. I have seen scores of them receive this promised blessing. And I can say of ourselves and the Africans, as Peter said of Jews and Gentiles, "He put no difference between us and them, purifying their hearts by faith."

c) "Am I Not a Christian?"

During one of our bushveld meetings, I stood at the altar and watched until there was a small pool of tears on the hard mud floor where a little woman dressed in skins, after the custom of the heathen, was kneeling. It was time for dismissal. It was also time for the Christian women to start to the neighboring heathen homes to invite the unsaved to come to the afternoon service. I knelt down to pray with the sobbing seeker, while the women started on their way, but the woman jumped up, shook out her cowskin skirt, and started toward the door. I called her back, and asked her where she was going. "Going!" she asked. "What do you mean? Am not I a Christian now? Am I not supposed to go and tell others about Jesus?" She had not been a Christian five minutes, but she was on her way to "bring others to the water that was not in the well."

It is not unusual for Swazi mothers in Africa to tie their babies on their backs and walk fifteen miles or more on Saturday, inviting heathen friends to the Sunday services. Even the little grandmas with stiff knee joints, walk many miles every week, witnessing to the power of Christ to save from heathen darkness. They sing choruses, quote verses of scripture, pray for the sick and troubled, and urge everyone to come to church.

On almost any Sunday morning when the sun peeps over the horizon, he finds the Christian boys and girls all washed and dressed in their Sunday best, and starting out to gather the heathen children in to the Sunday school.

d) Wanda.

Wanda was a very poor girl, but she always had an offering for her Lord. She usually put away most of the money she made during holidays to help support her pastor, and to pay her missionary dues. One time she had nothing to give. If she did not get some money this time, it would be the first time she had failed since she was converted. She prayed all week. On Saturday she decided that while the other girls went out to preach, she would work, if anyone would hire her. She offered her services for ten cents a day, so she would need to work two Saturdays in

order to have her shilling. On Saturday morning I
sent all the girls to the field to plow, for we were late
in planting that year. The girls sang and talked while
they worked, but Wanda kept on praying. When the
bell rang for the girls to quit work for the day, they
all grabbed their hoes and ran to the house. There
was one small piece of ground right in front of the
grinding shed that was not quite finished, so after the
girls were gone, Wanda decided to finish this little
plot, so they would not have to come back there Monday morning. As she dug, she prayed for her money,
telling God she had not failed Him, and she knew He
would not fail her, and that He would show her how
to get an offering for Him. As her hoe came down for
almost the last stroke, she saw something flat jump
up out of the earth. She stooped to see what it was,
and lo, it was an old silver shilling, dark with discolora-
tion. Wanda wept next day as she brought her coin,
now polished and bright, and she testified to the wonderful goodness and faithfulness of God who always
made a way for her.

Several years after her finding the coin, Wanda
died unexpectedly in a heathen kraal, but she sent
word by these kind people in whose home she died,
that God still helped her, even as she walked through
the valley of the shadow of death.

e) Grandmas.

Old Grandma Emely said God told her to go to a
week-end revival in an outstation, seventeen miles
from her home. I was leaving in the afternoon by

mule. I sent some of the schoolgirls in the morning, so they could walk along slowly with Grandma. We all arrived at dusk, and went into a night service. On Saturday we worked hard in a day service, and in kraal visiting, in preparation for the all night service which we planned for Saturday night. Emely prayed nearly all night with seekers, and testified two or three times. Sunday morning she went out to invite the near-by neighbors to the services. She entered with all her strength and soul into the services of the day— singing, shouting, praying and testifying. When the afternoon service was over, we prepared to leave for home. I thought that Grandma ought to wait and come home Monday; but she refused to be left behind. It was winter time. The sun went down, and a cold rain began to fall. It was so dark that we had to crawl on our hands and knees in places. There is a trail running around a side hill where once in the dark, Coffee (my mule) lost his footing and fell over the side with me on his back. When we came to this place, we began to feel our way along the narrow path. Someone slipped. I saw a white streak disappear below. I heard Grandma laugh, and shout from her place down the cliff: "Oh, girls, this isn't a fall. It is like being carried away in a river." By this time she had stopped sliding, and her cheery words sent the girls into screams of laughter. I was sure some of her bones were broken, and in my anxiety for her I fell into the hole of an ant bear (a good sized African animal which digs the hole in search of ants). But I came

out in double quick time when I heard a snakelike hissing in the side of the hole where my head was rammed.
We got ourselves out and over this place, but poor old
Grandma fell dozens of times, sometimes pulling us
down upon her. She never stopped her joking and
laughing. Then we waded a good-sized creek, where
the chill of the water made us shiver and shake. When
we reached the road where walking was safer, Grandma began to leap and praise God in a loud voice. As
she neared her home, she ran ahead to show us how
much strength she still had left. She declared that if
God needed her, she could go back over the same trip
the next day.

Emely will attempt anything. The harder the way,
the more fun she has, and she keeps on going. She
often goes to help dig a grave in the rain. This grave-
digging is about the least sought after of any work in
Africa. The heathen ask a whole cow to ceremoniously
cleanse those who help bury a dead person.

We had many little Grandmas who were great
workers for the Lord. I remember one who walked
all week to get to camp meeting. She came as far as
she could each day, and held a service at night among
the people of the kraal where she had asked to spend
the night. The Lord rewarded her by giving her souls
for her hire.

One old crippled woman, who could no longer go
with the women to preach, would crawl out to the trail
where she could preach to all the passers-by, during

the time the other women were visiting in the homes of the people.

Did not God promise that the people who love Him should bring forth fruit even in old age?

f) Esther's Motor Car.

"My car is the latest and best model," testified Esther, wife of Preacher Joseph. "In many ways it is a much better kind than the missionary's car." She went on to tell how her car excelled. She lived on a stony hill far away from a road, across several bridge-less rivers and deep gulches. She said, to begin with, her car did not cost much money. It did not eat petrol (gasoline). Then all she had to do to get to meeting was to gird it up and turn it loose. It ran down over the hill, following the narrow path, it slid over or around the rocks in the way; when it came to a river, it plunged in and *zizzed* out on the other side. She opened the throttle and sped through the veld in grass which was taller than the car itself. When she came to a gulch she tightened up the car's belt, scooted down the edge, and crawled up the steep bank on the other side. She came to the rancher's fence, and squeezed through and was carried safely and on time to the Preachers' Meeting. She thanked God for such a strong engine, for tires that did not wear out, and for beautiful equipment of every kind.

Note: This testimony was given by Esther shortly after Brother Schmelzenbach bought his first car. This was the only car owned by any of our missionaries at the time, and it was a great joy and wonder to our people. But Esther was a very zealous worker, and her description of her motor car referred to her long distance walks in connection with her work for the Master.

g) Healing of Jake's Mother.

Jake's mother lived alone in a little hut in Sabie Nook. She was a cripple, and had not taken a step in eleven years. She had spent all she had on native doctors, but was nothing bettered.

Mveli's mother, a kind neighbor, left a little bundle of sticks now and then with which Jake's mother could build a little open fire on which to cook the few grains of corn she could beg from her neighbors, and before which she might occasionally warm herself.

One day I was out kraaling (visiting in the homes of the people), and found Jake's mother, and was much moved by her sad story of pain, hunger, loneliness and sorrow. As I looked at her kind face, now deeply lined by marks of suffering, these words came again and again to my mind: "Then shall the lame man leap as an hart." That night as I prayed, I felt definitely that God wanted to save and heal my new-found friend.

The next day I took a bottle of anointing oil, and rode again up the Nook. On the way the enemy tried to tell me that she would not be healed. When I tried to bolster up my faith, the devil said, "Let not him that girdeth on his harness boast himself, as he that putteth it off." I stopped to pray and encourage myself in the Lord. Then I went on to my task. The poor woman said she chose Christ as her Saviour. I anointed her and prayed for her physical healing. That noon I left Sabie by train for a week's meeting in Swaziland. I prayed for this woman much that week, and when I returned, I went that very afternoon to see her. As I rode up the valley, and came to the place where I would follow the trail up the hill, I saw someone come from her little hut and start down the trail to meet me. As we approached each other, I saw that the one coming to meet me had a limp in her walk, and I wondered who she was. Then of a sudden the truth dawned upon me. It was Jake's mother, healed by the power of God. She said that after I left her the day I anointed and prayed for her, she thought to herself, "Now, if the Lord has healed me, I will get up and walk." She got up and had been walking about her home all the week. She was already preparing to take a long journey to visit her people whom she had not seen in many years. She made the long journey and returned safely.

h) He Lives Down Here.

The woman sat under the big tree and wept silently all through the service. When we were dismissed, I went to her and asked, "Mother, would you like to know the Jesus I have been telling you about?" She answered back, "I'm acquainted with Him." I looked at her. She was dressed in mourning, with a long necklace of medicine and charms hanging around her neck. "You know Jesus!" I exclaimed. She an-

swered, "I know Him. He lives here at Lubisana."
Then she told me that she saw Him by her child when
she was sick, and that she often met Him at her
child's grave. She said she often went to the grave,
because her heart rested there where Jesus stayed.

I had seen this Christian daughter-in-law a few
days before she died. She was sick of malaria, and
they had waited too long to call us. She lay on the old
grass mat under a shade made of goatskins. It was
midsummer, and the flies hovered about in clouds. She
was a mass of running sores from the top of her head
to the soles of her feet. They had cut all the hair
from her head, and were trying the best they knew
how to take care of her. Flies lined her eyelids,
crawled in and out of her mouth and nose, and over
the running sores. She was almost gone. We saw her
lips moving. I thought perhaps she had seen me, and
had some little message for me. I stooped down and
listened. Then I heard her saying over and over,
"Jesus, Jesus, precious Jesus." I came away feeling
that I too had met Jesus there.

i) The Hailstorm.

We had about two hundred hungry mouths to feed
at the Schmelzenbach Memorial Station. There were
the witch babies, homeless and orphan children, the
native workers, the old grandmas and the women who
had been chased away from home by witchcraft, all
looking for food from our fields.

The crop was good that year. The corn and other
foods were just about ready to eat. The trees were

full of fruit. We were so thankful for our almost two hundred acres of beautiful gardens. But on that very hot December afternoon, I looked up suddenly to find the heavens black with stormclouds. A great, green cloud was swiftly coming our way. I could hear strange, clattering sounds in the heavens, and knew that meant hail! A real storm this time. I had seen the hail beat beautiful fields of food to the ground, and the rain wash even the stocks away, until the fields looked like land after the spring plowing. I had seen the storm break huge limbs off trees, smash all the window panes in our buildings, and cast stones as large as small hen eggs at the occupants inside. I had gazed in horror as I saw the speedy destruction of fowls, animals, food and property before the terrible rage of such a storm. Fear clutched my heart. I looked at our beautiful fields that we must reap if we kept our large family together. I sat down quickly on the porch, for I could stand no longer. Just then from the little mud-walled home in which I lived with my big family of girls came a sudden volume of mighty, desperate prayer. Immediately my fright gave place to confidence. I knew God could not turn a deaf ear to such pleading. Alice had seen the storm before I saw it, and had marshaled the girls to bring help from the only One who is able to deliver in such a crisis. He did not fail those Swazi girls. A sharp wind from the opposite direction sprang up in just a minute of time and drove the storm past our fields. It stripped every leaf from the trees, pulverized the grass, tore off huge limbs from the trees, and left a path of utter destruction in its wake, but not an ear of corn was damaged in our fields. God had taken our gardens into His care.

3. *Unusual Methods.*

a) "Turn the orange loose."

Alice, the evangelist, was praying and exhorting among the girls who were at the altar seeking to be forgiven or to receive the Holy Spirit. She was urging some to pray. Others she exhorted to put their trust in the Lord. But coming to one girl, who was especially hesitant, Alice called out in great earnestness, "Turn the orange loose, and God will bless you." This I afterward found to be a rather favorite form of exhortation among our native evangelists, and I found it also convenient and effective for my own purposes.

The metaphor is drawn from a very familiar practice in trapping monkeys. Monkeys are a pest in Africa, especially to those who have vegetable gardens or gardens of peanuts. The monkeys are fond of about all kinds of vegetables which are used for human food, and in addition to their gathering for their own use, they are destructive of vines and plants. The children, especially the boys, are assigned the task of minding the monkeys away from the gardens. But of course this is monotonous work, and various means are used for making the work more effective and exciting.

One kind of native monkey trap is very ingenious. a good-sized, long handled gourd is used as the main part of the trap. The gourd is fastened with grass cords to some nearby stake or tree. A small hole is made in the shell of the gourd. A few peanuts and a small, bright colored orange are placed inside the gourd. Peanuts or other monkey delicacies are used for bait, being strewn about the location of the gourd on the ground. The monkeys usually go about in companies. When such a company approaches the trap, the monkeys are led on by the scattered peanuts, and finally come to the gourd itself. One of the bolder ones of the group reaches in and takes out a peanut. Emboldened by his initial success, he finally grasps the orange, which by reason of its bright color has attracted his attention. But with his hand grasped about the orange, the monkey's fist is too large to be withdrawn from the gourd. The monkey becomes greatly excited, but he never thinks to "turn the orange loose." He labors to free himself, and his friends come to his assitance. These friends lay hold upon the arm of the fastened monkey, and pull with all their might. The chattering and screaming draws the attention of the men and boys in the nearby kraal, and they come and kill the monkey and any of his friends which are too slow in fleeing. But all the time, the whole story could have been changed, if the monkey had just "turned the orange loose"; for then his hand could have been withdrawn from the gourd without difficulty.

To the native African, the seeker after God who holds fast to his sins or fails to make a complete con-

secration of all his ransomed powers appears at once
as the human imitator of the foolish monkey who will
not "turn the orange loose."

　　b) "Have You Sent Back All that Belongs to
　　　　Him?"

The African young people who are in the transi-
tion between the old heathen ways and the new Christian ways have many methods of their own. Take
their courtships: A young man may just hear of a
young woman in some other part of the country whom
he thinks he would like for a wife. If he can make
arrangements to do so, he will go by for just a look at
her. In our mission stations it often happens that a
young man will ask to go to one of the other stations
on some more or less unimportant errand. We know
why he wants to make the trip, and so make arrangements for it. At the station he makes no effort to en-
gage the young woman in conversation, and is con-
tent if it is made possible for him to just see the desired
one as she passes through the room or across the mission compound. Sometimes just by this passing glimpse
he makes up his mind whether or not she is the one he
wants. If he decides she is the one, the courtship is
carried on pretty much by letters. He writes the girl
a very complimentary note in which he tells of her
beauty, and of his high regard for her. As expected,
there is no response from the girl. After a short wait,
he writes again: this time making his plea much more
forceful. Still there is no answer. The third letter becomes almost frantic, and the loveliness of the girl is

extolled beyond all metaphors, and the love of the young man is declared in extravagant terms.

Now it is time for the girl to make some response. But this response is likely to be simply, "I cannot hear what you say." This is an invitation to the young man to write again with better words and fuller sentences. After awhile the girl responds, "I cannot hear what *that one* says. Perhaps if he could speak more plainly, I could hear." This is the signal for the fullest proposal the young man can make. When that letter comes, the young woman must make some reply. In that reply, if the girl wants him, she will tell him something to make him understand. She may say, "I cannot see this, but if you see it, it is all right. Then the young man writes her a letter of thanks, and sends her a silk handkerchief for her to wear on her head as a sign of their engagement.

But if the young woman finds herself unconcerned, she will write back and say, "Excuse me, friend. I am sorry. I do not like you. Do not write me any more." And in connection with this note, if she really means what she says, she returns all the letters she has received from the young man, and the suit is closed.

But if, as is sometimes the case, the young woman does not really want to close the matter for good, but does want to teach the young man that he will have to work hard to get such a girl as she is, she will return his package of letters and tell him not to write any more. But she holds back one of his letters or even just a portion of one of his letters. The young man looks through the package when he receives it, and if he finds that the young woman has not returned absolutely everything he has ever sent her, he takes it that she is not really through, and so he goes on with his love making. She may act as though she strongly objects to his letters, may make a scene among her friends, may even send other letters back unopened, but if the young man wants her, he will keep right on. If she has now decided she does not want the man, she is afraid to produce the letter which she withheld, for it is evidence that she did want him and was playing with him. It will not help her to burn the letter—it must be returned. In the end if the young man is called in question for troubling the young woman, he will finally tell them that she kept his letter. If he can prove this, the fault returns upon the girl. She will be told that by her acts she has engaged herself to the young man. If she now refuses to accept him, she will be given punishment. I have known such an act to be cause for removing the young woman from the class of full members in the church, and to require her to stay for months in the probationers' class.

It often happens that when some chronic seeker fails to trust God for salvation, and seems to hesitate in decision, the African evangelist or lay worker will cry out, "Have you sent back every single thing that belongs to him?" The whole picture comes up to the seeker, and he knows it means that he is to get rid of every offending thing: that he must clear out everything that belongs to the devil and to the world or else the fault of his want of victory will come home upon his own head.

c) A Dream—The Little Gray Hands.

One morning the wife of the medicine man, Koza, came early to the Sabie Mission Station to ask prayer. She too had practiced native medicine before she gave her heart to the Lord, but she had a wonderful conversion. During the first months of her Christian life she had walked very close to God. For some time, however, she had not been so faithful in attendance at prayer meeting, in testimony and in Christian service. We were troubled about her, and feared she might go back into heathenism. But that morning she said that God had given her a wonderful dream which made her very much afraid. She had come to get help for her soul. Three times in succession she dreamed that Jesus had come back to the earth for His people. She saw the city of God with its shining gates wide open. Long lines of people were marching into the city. Every marcher was arrayed in a beautiful white gown. Each wore a glittering crown, and all were waving feathery branches and singing happy songs of praise and triumph. She was very excited and happy.

Then came the Christians with whom she worshiped in her church, and she thought it was now time for her to get into line with the others. She watched as they drew near, and tried to get up to take her place with the others, but she could neither get up nor move. Finally she got her eyes off the wonderful scene, and began to get excited about herself. She looked at her dress that had been washed so clean and white, and now it was badly soiled. She wondered how she had been so careless. She struggled to free herself, but found herself absolutely immovable. She noticed that there were some little hands on her, so she brushed them off. But as these let go, scores of other little hands grabbed her. She said these hands were the size of the feet of baby mice, and that they were gray in color. None of them were very black— just gray. None were very strong, but there were so many of them that they held her as fast as though she had been bound with leather ropes.

After she had dreamed this same dream three times, she began to hear what God was saying to her. She had been washed clean in the blood of Jesus. But she had been careless of her clean garments. She had not done anything really black and bad, but she had neglected God and His service. She had done some little questionable things. It was not that any of the hands were very strong, but there were so many of them. It confused her. She wanted us to come immediately and help her to get Jesus to take away the little gray hands, and wash her dress and make it white again.

After this experience she often talked to the people about soiled clothes and little gray hands. She told the Christians to brush everything off every night before they went to sleep. She had learned, she said, that little things will keep people out of the City of God, and she did not want others to learn this by the terrible experience that she had suffered. Little sins. she said, will tie a person so he cannot get to God just as surely as big sins, like beer drinking and fighting will do.

NOTE—Most of the Africans are illiterate—especially the women. They have so little to help them in their Christian lives, and they get very little from the Bible. It is perhaps because of these things that God seems often to use dreams to teach them wonderful Bible lessons.

4. *Giving.*

a) Hosea's Tickey.

Hosea had a tickey (a little coin worth about five cents) hid away in her soap box trunk. She went to get it for the big offering. She saw her new Sunday dress that her mother had just bought her. Hosea's parents were Christians. Most of the girls had only their school clothes made of calico. This light colored dress was very dear to Hosea's heart. As she fingered it tenderly, God said to this little Swazi girl, "I don't want your tickey, Hosea, I want your dress." This was one of the hardest tests that had ever come to Hosea. Finally, she took the garment that to her was so beautiful, carried it down to the church, and laid it on the altar. God sanctified Hosea in that meeting. For a few months she was a bright and shining light. Then sickness came to our home, and little Hosea lay unconscious for many days. Then God took her to live with Him. He took away her cheap dress that He might give her a shining robe.

b) Anna's Bed.

We were taking an offering to build a church in which the students were much interested. They had been praying and fasting, and asking God to somehow supply the need. With shining faces they began to bring their offerings. One gave the one and only little goat she ever owned. Another gave her last chicken. Tema, whose parents are heathen, had a hard time to keep her body covered with even a ragged dress. But she gave her dress. It was old and worn, and worth only a few pennies at the most, but it was her best.

Anna, who is not too bright mentally, but who knew God thoroughly, and who spent hours daily praying while others were in school, thought she had nothing to give, and was heartbroken. All the other girls made grass mats, but Anna's mats just wouldn't seem to make. Lillian had given her a very beautiful and neatly woven sleeping mat. This was Anna's only earthly possession, and of it she was very proud. We saw Anna get up and leave the church building. After a few minutes she came back with her sleeping mat in her arms. She was smiling triumphantly, and patting her mat. As she placed her gift on the altar, we were all greatly moved, for we knew how Anna loved her beautiful mat, and that she would have no bed that night, only as other girls shared their mats with her. I wrote to friends in Santa Ana, California, about Tema's dress and Anna's bed, and they sent a nice dress and money to get a sleeping mat. I saw God supply the needs of those girls from most unimaginable sources, saw Him do mighty works of grace in their hearts and lives, saw Him save their loved ones and make the girls a blessing to very many. When all the goats, mats, hens, pigs, dresses, etc., were sold, we had in this one offering over five hundred dollars from the one little day school.

c) Goat Meat for Stamps.

Fifty schoolgirls had one little goat for meat each two weeks. This meat was used for soup or to help the porridge or sweet potatoes to go down. They had some girl friends in Santa Ana, California, to whom they wanted to send some little mats and baskets which they had worked hard to prepare. They wanted stamps to mail their parcels, so they sold the goat for money to buy postage and did without meat for an extra two weeks. It was winter time, so there were no green weeds or vegetables with which to make *umshibo* (gravy). Their diet for the month between goat meat supplies was almost entirely corn meal porridge.

d) Blessings in Tithing.

One Sunday morning I saw a little heathen Swazi woman trudging up the hill toward the church. She carried a well filled sack on her head. I called to her and said, "Where are you going on Sunday, Mother, with your heavy load?" "Me, Daughter of the King," she answered, "I saw the children of God taking in the tithe of their fields and coming away happy. I'm bringing in my peanuts because I too want to be happy."

e) Alice's Goats.

Alice had a few goats. She left them with her sister who was not a Christian. Sometimes the other goats of the flock died of sickness, but Alice's goats always escaped. They multiplied rapidly. When other goats bore only single kids, hers often bore twins. After Alice paid the tithe of her goats, she gave offerings of goats. When visiting preachers came, I have known her to kill as many as three goats in one day to feed these hungry servants of God. Although she was so liberal, she always had a few more goats. I have heard her testify many times about these wonderful animals. She thinks it would not be often that sickness or thieves would touch God's goats. She challenges the natives to prove for themselves that this is a profitable way to doctor their live stock against sickness and theft.

f) Lukele's Tithe of Corn.

Lukele was a new convert. He had just heard for the first time that the tithe belongs to God. He had a wife and one child. His garden had yielded little corn for the winter. He felt that he should measure out the tithe of his corn and take it to his Swazi preacher. He looked at the four sacks of food, all that stood between his family and starvation, and decided he would wait for a better crop before he began to pay his tithe. After a short time Lukele started out to look for work. On the way he tried to pray that God would lead him

to the right place. He did not make much progress
with his prayer, for he was ashamed to ask very much
of God. His heart kept saying within him, "You have
robbed God. You would not steal your neighbor's
corn, but you have stolen corn from God. How can
you, a thief, ask God to help you find work?"

Lukele met a man who was going back to his
neighborhood, so he sent a message to his wife, Ella,
telling her that he had met God on the way, that he
saw he had stolen corn, and that she should take the
corn that did not belong to him, and to add to it to
make the sack full, and give it to the preacher. Ella
took the corn to the Swazi preacher. Lukele found a
good job. In a few months he came home to do his
spring planting. I heard him testify and tell how he
stole God's corn, but returned it with the added gift.
And he said, "this year I planted the same fields in
the same way, and reaped ten sacks of corn where I
never reaped more than four before." Lukele proved
God and got the poured out blessings.

g) An Object Lesson in Tithing.

We were giving the churches lessons in tithing. We
went to one of the outstations to meet all the Christians of that zone. We had sacks, tin cans, dishes and
cups with which to demonstrate the way in which to
separate the tithe of all their produce. Swazies have
little money. But during reaping time they designate
one Sunday on which to bring all their tithe of corn.
Another Sunday they bring pumpkins, fruit and like
produce. On another Sunday they bring their dif-

ferent kinds of beans, peanuts, etc. Then there is a day
for bringing the tithe of all their fowls and animals.
If they get money they bring the tithe of that immediately. Or they may bring all the tithe of their produce
on the same day. We did this once at Endingeni. We
had three oxen, three goats, twenty-one chickens,
more than twenty sacks of corn, and many sacks of
peanuts and beans. There were dishes large and small
filled with every kind of foodstuffs. There were large
bunches of bananas, rolls of grass mats, and bundles
of grass brooms and grass ropes. Some old women
who had nothing to tithe, had gathered from the bush
huge bundles of firewood, and had carried these in on
their heads. It was a very impressive sight to see all
the tithe piled up in the storehouse that Sunday morning.

Tithes are sold and the money used to help support
the national workers of the local church bringing in
the produce. Natives who have never had even a
simple lesson in arithmetic learn quickly, when they
are shown by object lessons how the tithe is separated.
This was the reason for our gathering at Empondhla.

We read our scripture lesson from Malachi. Several had testified as to how God blessed and increased
them, after they began to tithe, and we had stressed
God's promise of blessing to all who would bring the
tithe into the storehouse, and thus prove Him. We
were progressing nicely with our object lessons. One,
then another poured corn and beans into sacks, tins
and dishes or separated a tithe from the pumpkins.

Then a woman stood up in the rear of the building, and asked the privilege of telling us about her troubles with tithing. She gave us a story that went like this: "I want to tell you, good teachers, my story. Too, I want to ask what you think about this great thing that came upon me. My preacher told me about paying God one part out of every ten parts. I heard him well. I had only one hen. She laid ten eggs and hatched out nine chicks. Now I had my red hen and nine chicks—ten in all. It was time for me to think about my tithe this year. When the day came for us to bring in our tithes, I took one of those chicks and gave it to my preacher. When I came home I found an animal had killed all eight of the remaining chickens. How do you explain that?"

The preachers and I tried to comfort her, and to fix it up the best we could. There were so many questions asked that it took up all the remaining time. We were troubled. Our time was gone. Our object lesson was forgotten by all. Those many Christians would go home to tell their people about those dead chickens of the woman who was faithful to bring in her tithe. Our whole trip had been worse than in vain. We stood up to be dismissed. The same woman spoke out again, and said, "There is a bit more I want to tell you teachers. Yes, I had a red hen. She hatched out nine chicks. They grew fast and big. Only one of them did not grow so big as the others. It was a little sick. When I looked at my chickens I picked out the biggest and best, and said to my heart that I should

take that one for the Lord. But I had two hearts. One
was a big heart, and one was a little heart. The little
heart said I better take the little chicken. It said, 'One
is a tenth, big or little. If you keep the big chicken,
you will have many big chickens to give God next
year. The preacher will only eat your chickens. Meat
is meat. All the difference would be that there would
not be so much meat.' My big heart refused. When it
came tithe day, my little heart overcame my big heart.
I took the little chicken. When I got home the others
were dead. In every kraal of our people—those who
are not Christians—we always give the biggest and
best ox to the spirits. We give them the best of all we
have. The great God-Spirit gave me more rest and
joy in this little time since I chose Him than I ever
had in all the years I served the many spirits that our
people worship. I know it is a shame for me to offer
the great God presents that I would be afraid to offer
to the spirits. After this, I will give God the best part
of what I have." The day was saved. By her little
story this woman had taught everyone, big and little,
in that whole congregation more than we could have
taught them had we a whole week in which to try.

　h) *Umbongo.*

Every year at the big camp meeting we have an
offering that the natives call *umbongo.* It is strictly a
native way of taking an offering. It takes a long time
to get such an offering started. But we have a lot of
time, for the offering usually continues throughout
the night.

After the money has been collected to take care of the expenses of the meeting, the *umbongo* begins. One of the preachers usually starts off by standing up front and telling of some unusual thing the Lord has done for him during the year. Then he says, "Words are cheap. This time I will say, 'Thank you, Lord,' with something stronger than words. I have at home a little thing—a small rooster. It is not enough. It is nothing. But I will say, 'Thank you, Lord,' by this four-legged rooster." All the congregation say in a loud voice, "Amen!" His little rooster is probably a big ox. Another man will come forward with a small square of cowhide. When he has told of his special blessings, he says his thanks with the cowhide which he lays on the altar. This is another ox. Another man will come with a little wisp of hair from a cow's tail. He makes a clever speech, never mentioning the animal which the hair represents. He gives it another name, but all know that he is giving an ox. He mentions the day that he will drive the gift up to the one who will care for the offerings. A woman waves a chicken feather: that means a chicken. Every time one lays his offering on the altar, the people call out loudly, "Amen!" Even the children are disappointed if they are not given an opportunity to stand up alone and thank the Lord. I have seen scores of small children each bring an egg, a few peanuts or sweet potatoes or corn in both their little hands, and, like the others, say, "With this, I thank you, Lord." I have seen dozens of old women each take out some small objects, perhaps a big safety pin from their shawl (such a pin is a real treasure), or take off their colored handkerchief—their Sunday hat—and lay their gifts upon the altar. They pile up sacks of peanuts and corn, and piles of squash and citrons. They put the feathers, hair, pieces of hoof or hide, coins and all the things that have been brought in and laid upon the altar together to be counted. When one once sees a real *umbongo,* he will never forget it. All the gifts are gathered together and sold, and the proceeds are put with the money. Such offerings are usually used for building a new church building somewhere.

i) Men and Missions.

Perhaps you would like to hear about "Men and Missions" in Africa. Swazi men do not like to belong to anything run entirely by women, so they have a missionary organization of men. There is nothing that can disgrace an African man more than to say of him, "He is a woman." There is no way to so praise a woman as to say she is a man.

Most of our Christian men belong to the missionary organization, and pay their money regularly. Preacher Jacobe and his men of Sherrow Chapel high up in the mountains, decided they did not want to just pay the same as the women of their church for Missions, so each man brought twice the amount asked of the women. They said, since they were men, they were not going to give like women. Also, they took the territory farthest from home as their field to evangelize. Since they were men, and it meant a lot to them to put forth this extra effort, God blessed them in a remarkable way.

It is the plan for the Missionary Society of our field to open and support work in a new field where our missionaries have not been. Thus our Nazarenes of Africa will have a foreign missionary task of their own.

j) Making Money Talk.

I have known a woman to walk seventy miles to sell her last chicken or a little bag of corn or a clay pot to get money for her missionary offering. I have, time and again, seen little old women kneel at the altar, and holding up a shilling, pray like this: "Lord, put a mouth in this money of mine, and let it preach the gospel w-a-y over there where my voice cannot be heard. Put hands on this money of mine, Lord, and let them work for me w-a-y over there where my hands cannot reach. Lord, put feet on this shilling of mine, and let them run errands for Thee w-a-y over there where my feet cannot be."

k) Not Ready to Die.

Grandma seemed to be dying. For days she lingered at the entrance of the valley. But she seemed distressed. Her family heard her say over and over, "I'm not ready to die. I'm not ready to die." Finally her heathen brothers sat down beside her and said, "Now, sister, you said you were a child of God. You told us that if we would believe on God, we would no longer be afraid of death. You have preached everywhere that you were ready to go to God's City. You

will not let us bring the witch doctor to heal you. And
yet today you cause us pain. You make us wonder
greatly. You fight and struggle and roll on your mat.
Tell us, sister, what must we do for you?" Then she
told them that she had a debt. She could not die and
leave a debt. They could understand that of course,
for Christians pay their debts. She asked them if they
would take her goat—she had just one, a big kid—and
try to sell it for her. While they went on their way,
Grandma prayed that they might find a buyer. They
found a buyer who gave them five shillings for the
goat. When Grandma got her money she told her
brothers she would send them just one time more before she moved into her new home. She laid one
shilling on the mat, and said, "Take this to my preacher, and tell him this is my debt for my missionary dues
this quarter." She laid out the second shilling, and
said, "Take this to my preacher and tell him this is for
the next quarter for my missionary dues. She put out
the third and fourth coins and told them to tell the
preacher these were for the third and fourth quarters.
She kept the last shilling for herself. Then she looked
up and smiled, and said to those gathered about her,
"Won't I feel wonderful when I see Jesus?" She rolled
over and went to sleep, her troubled tossing over. She
had paid her missionary dues, and was now ready to
go whenever Jesus called for her.

   5. *Building.*

We needed a dispensary building very badly. Our
little, old huts of mud and poles where we cared for the

sick were falling down on us. They were so small
that we had no room for tables or beds. Our patients,
no matter how sick, lay on mud or cement floors. One
stormy night a woman was very ill. The rain beat into
our hut and made great puddles on the cement floor
on which this woman was lying. We pulled the woman
on her mat from one corner of the hut to the other
until all the places were drenched. At last we raised
two umbrellas over the sick one while Nurse Beta
and I kneeled for hours on the cold cement and worked
to save a life. That night I made a decision. I would
build some new buildings for our medical work. We
had no money with which to build. It would be too
expensive to make burned bricks. Down in the bottom of a canyon, not far from the mission home, our
native builder, Enoch, had found a lot of building
stone. The sides of the hill were too steep for the
oxen to go all the way down, so most of the stones
would have to be carried out on the heads of women.
I sent word to all our neighbors, Christian and heath-
en, that on Friday and Saturday we would carry stones
to make a "Medicine House." Friday morning at daybreak, Mrs. Mischke and I went with the girls and
women, little Richard Mischke went with the children,
and Mr. Mischke went with the big boys and men.
About 250 women carried large stones on their heads
up the steep side of the canyon. Among these women
was one demon doctor, who came because her chief
ordered all his people to be there for work. When this
woman's head got tired, she laughingly remarked that

the demons refused to work for the Christians. The
men dug the stones out and placed them on the heads
of the carriers. Others came with their ox or donkey
drawn sledges as far down the hillside as possible, and
drew out hundreds of loads of stone. Some of the
boys took stones from the top to the building site by
wagon. We stopped at noon for lunch made of one ox
and cornmeal porridge. After a short service, we went
back to wrestle with stones until sundown. We were
all so sore and bruised that I felt sure nobody would
come back for work the next day. The next morning
I limped out and went with the girls from the Girls'
Home back to the work. I did not expect anyone to
come, and only went to work a short time because I
had said we would work on Saturday. As we drew
near the stone pile, I was amazed to find the place
black with waiting heathen. There were more men,
more oxen and more sledges than there had been the
day before. We got more and bigger stones out of more
difficult places than we had done on Friday. God
worked with us that day. We sang and shouted all over
the hillside, and everybody had lots of fun. Our weari-
ness vanished, our lunch of sweet potatoes was especially good, and everybody went home that night
satisfied with himself and everything in general.
There was by now a huge pile of building stone ready
to be trimmed and used. In just two days we had
brought out half the stone required for the building.

The government gave us large, straight eucalyptus
poles for the roof. The men cut and hauled these, and

treated them with a tar preparation to keep out the
white ants. The women for miles about cut long roofing grass. Scores of bundles of grass were carried for
a distance of fifteen miles on the heads of women and
children. Irish Peter did a wonderful job on the stone
work, and Willie, my first orphan boy, did a beautiful
job with the grass roof. Children who had been raised
in the home, but who now had positions as teachers,
cooks or housekeepers paid for the material to make
tables, cupboards, bed boxes, baby beds, etc., and
Willie made all this equipment.

When the building was completed, with its circle
of round native huts in the back, we had a great dedication day. The Principal Medical Officer of Swaziland came to open the building. Most of the white
population, and great throngs of natives came to rejoice with us. Everybody brought a gift. There were
hundreds of mats, baskets, brooms, clay pots, wooden
spoons, large washpans, etc., brought by the natives.
The white guests brought hot water bags, instruments,
hospital gowns, etc. We served tea to the white guests
on our pretty vine covered veranda. The natives had
ready many huge clay pots full of meat, and a big vat
of cornmeal porridge. We had a wonderful day, and
moved into our new set of buildings that had been
made possible with very little money, but by much
help from many friends, and the leadership and blessings of our mighty God.

There are very few builders in our part of Africa.
Material is expensive and scarce. We usually make

our buildings on the main stations of burned brick or
cement blocks, and roof them with corrugated iron.
The outstation chapels, school buildings, and dispensaries are made of native stone pointed with cement, and are roofed with tile or a good kind of grass.

It fell to my lot to build many buildings during my
stay in Africa. I always greatly enjoyed this work.
We always paid as we built, never going into debt. I
have often dug sand all day along with natives who
were almost discouraged from working alone so long,
and without pay. I have stood for hours in a mud-
hole molding brick, teaching the boys and girls how
the work is done. I have splashed myself with mud
from head to heels as I raced the natives in mud
plastering a worker's home. For my work as a builder,
the Swazies gave me another "praise name"—*Uno-
maka*—meaning *skillful builder*.

6. *Revival Methods*

a) Swazi Revivals.

Our revival meetings usually begin on Thursday
and run over Sunday. The meetings are short, but in-
tense. Such meetings are always preceded by much
prayer and fasting. Christians from surrounding
churches always come in numbers to help in these
meetings. There is always one whole night of prayer.
The Christians have the first part of the meeting to
get themselves revived and blessed. Saturday night
and all day Sunday are usually given to efforts to win
the unsaved. There is never enough room for the people. I have seen as many as three hundred heathen

boys sit packed together on the floor all night. They always reminded me of a flock of young mountain goats on a lark. It often took over an hour to get them under control so the preacher could bring the message. They used to wear me completely out, until I learned to turn them over to the Swazies.

I remember one meeting when we had several hundred more people than could possibly be seated on the floor in closest Swazi fashion. We did not know what to do, so we had them ring the bell for the service. When they began to come in, I told them to all stand. The only seats were a row of benches around the edge where the big men would sit. I had the people to crowd in as close as they could stand, until all were inside the door. Then I called out, *"Hlalani pansi"* (Be seated)! Everybody sat quick, knowing that all would not get a place. A howl of laughter filled the room. Scores of little eyes peered out from under the benches around the edge of the room. Three young women sat under the little table before me. I could not move my feet an inch, for they were covered with children. They were two deep all through the middle of the building, but everybody was down one way or another, except one man who could not make it in any direction at all. He had been working in the mines, had bought himself a new hat, and was all decked out in colors that evening. His special purpose at the meeting was to have a look at the pretty girls and choose one that he might ask permission to write her and try to win her. The girls knew all this, so it was especially funny that he should be the one who could not get down. He wiggled to the right and to the left, all the young men trying to help him. Little by little he began to sink. But as he went down, his arm came up, for there was not room for all of him in that little space. In his upraised hand he held his new hat. Everybody was watching him. Miss Lovelace spoke up to say, "It will soon be all right, brethren, he is all gone now but his hat." With this speech, we tried no longer to keep from laughing.

A big crowd, blessings upon the Christians, and heathen choosing the Lord is what constitutes a good Swazi revival.

b) Prayer Huts.

For twenty years or so we have had one or more prayer huts on the Schmelzenbach Memorial Station. These are huts set aside to be used only by people who want a place to pray undisturbed. Some years everyone on the station has a set period once a week when he is alone in the prayer hut. At other times, the girls have the daytime, and the boys the night. At still other times all who want to participate are given an hour, so that for weeks at a time, day and night, somebody is always praying in the prayer hut. One does not leave until the next one comes to take his place. Many of the victories we have had on this station, and on the district have been won beforehand in the prayer hut. Today the girls have a hut called The Florence Davis Prayer Hut. The boys have The Stephen's Prayer Hut near their sleeping quarters. The girls'

hut was named for Mrs. Florence Davis of Colorado,
and the boys' hut for Stephen Sherros of Richmond,
Indiana. Both these have been great friends and faithful supporters of this work. The missionaries also
have their prayer hut where they can steal away from
their cares and labors, and from the presence of the
people to spend some time alone with God. Most mission stations have prayer huts, and it is impossible to
overestimate the blessing they have been to our
African work. They are the power houses that have
broken the bands of wickedness, and transformed
darkness into light.

c) Three Days of Fasting and Prayer.

It was in the darkest days of the depression. Money
was very scarce, and national workers were face to
face with such a period of adjustment as they had
never known before. Above all, there had been crop
failure, and many were hungry. It sometimes seemed
to them that they must leave their God-appointed
tasks and take up secular work to supply their many
needs. Because of the many things hard to be understood, it was easy for a spirit of misunderstanding to
creep in between the workers, and between the national workers and the missionaries. Try as we might,
every new discussion seemed only to widen the gulf.
It came to the place where we went to every new
meeting with fear and trembling, and would come
away knowing that we had made no progress toward
the solution of our problems. Finally, after much
prayer and waiting on God, I sent word to all the

workers of the Pigg's Peak area that we were going to
a certain outstation to have three days of fasting and
waiting in prayer before the Lord. All the national
workers were invited. They could come or stay at
home—just as they pleased. They could bring food,
if they cared to, but no cooking was to be done on the
station for anybody. On Thursday evening about fifty
national workers, Fairy Chism, Irene Jester and I
gathered in the little stone church building at Hele-
hele, and began to wait on God. There was little progress for many hours. Then Preacher Simon crawled
over to Evangelist Solomon and suggested that he ask
the missionaries if it would be all right for them to
send their possessions over the brook Jabok, so they
might be unencumbered in their wrestling. They
stood up one by one and began confessing little things
that had been troubling them in their hearts. Criticism, hard feelings, careless words whose hurt they
had made room for in their hearts, a lack of that love
and confidence they had once felt for fellow workers.
A recess was called, and all over the church and prem-
ises they gathered by twos or in little groups, and
talked freely, explaining and asking forgiveness. We
all joined together in getting everything across the
brook. Finally, with smiling faces, and with hearts at
rest with men, we went back to God in prayer. He
met with us in a wonderful manner. The gulf disappeared. The financial burdens shriveled up to the
size a man could carry. The tall mountains of hard-
ship and fear wore low until the rugged path was such

as a brave soldier could follow. We prayed for our part of the work, for the district, for the whole church, and for special projects. We prayed for the children of all our workers, calling them by name. We had a healing service, and prayed for the bodies of the sick among us. Some of the testimonies were very good. One preacher had been sure he would die of hunger. He was ashamed to bring his food to the station, so he had hidden a handful of food out in the veld, intending to go and eat it just before he starved to death. He had become so interested that he had never once felt either hungry or thirsty. Another man, not strong in body, decided to stay home Thursday night, and come up to the meeting on Friday morning. This would give him one good meal on the first day. His wife cooked a big chicken with plenty of sweet potatoes and other food to fortify him for one day at least. Very early in the morning he arose from a troubled sleep, saying, "The soldiers are in battle, why do I hide at home like a coward?" Much to the dismay of his wife, he sneaked off and left the meat and potatoes untouched in the pot. He walked more than fifteen miles, joined the army, and stayed to pray and shout until the last minute of the battle.

It was past midnight on Sunday when we finished all we had to do. Even then, the Swazies did not go to sleep. They laughed and talked while the women leisurely prepared the food. At daybreak they ate a hearty meal. Then all joined hands, sang a battle song, and asked, "Why didn't you do this long ago?"

d) The Meeting at Nhlangiyavuka.

We wanted to help this little home missionary church. It was well located in the deep bushveld among hundreds of kraals. During the winter the people spent their time at beer drinks, and did not seem to know why we had built our little church down there. Six or eight preachers, a group of girls from the school, some interested lay members and I all went down to this little outstation church for a ten days meeting. We visited in the homes of the people all during the days, and had services at night. The water was scarce and bad. I boiled the milky liquid, and threw in some tea leaves to change the odor. There had been a crop failure. The only food in the neighborhood was kaffir corn. Natives, missionaries and animals all ate kaffir corn until I thought I'd never want to see any more red porridge as long as I lived. We gained the attention and friendship of almost everybody in the neighborhood. God heard our prayers and gave us a bountiful harvest, with several score professing to find salvation. We left a teacher, and opened a day school for the children.

e) Revival at Enzulase.

The preaching was anointed of God. Message after message of unusual type was delivered. A whole night was spent in fasting and prayer. We were in our last service, and still the church had not been blessed nor the heathen moved. We had many reasons to know that God had been leading us in this battle. The native Christians will do what their leaders tell them to do. I was so sure that God was trying to do something for us that in that last service I told the church we would begin our meeting all over again: have another night of prayer, preach and pray again, and wait until God at least blessed His people. This was such an unusual procedure that some got stirred. They began to talk. Finally one young, timid girl stood up and said that God had been condemning her for not telling us why the church was not blessed. As she began to talk, others joined in, and we found there had been a quarrel in which most of the church members were involved, and that some had even accused others of practicing witchcraft. Hours of talking followed—a real native *indaba*. In the end, the people asked forgiveness of one another, and fixed up their difficulties. Most of the church went to the altar, and soon came up with smiling faces. It was not long until the atmosphere had completely changed. The blessings of God were showered richly upon us, and several heathen stood, lifted up their right hands, and cried, "*Ngiyayiket 'iNkosi*" (I choose the Lord). We were glad we had not struck once and stopped (II Kings 13: 18, 19). We were taught the lesson of striking on and on until we consumed our enemies.

f) The Big Meeting.

We enlisted every Christian. We divided the surrounding territory for a distance of eight miles in every direction into different sections that could be reached in one day by one group. We divided the people into groups. Every home in every section was visited daily

for over a week by one or more Christians. These
visitors sang, gave a little message, invited the people
to church, prayed, and pressed those who showed conviction to yield themselves to the Lord. At night we
spent hours in prayer for the ones we had visited in
the daytime. A cold wind came that kept the people
in their huts, so we found a wonderful opportunity to
preach Christ to them daily. As mighty conviction
settled down, the whole neighborhood became excited
and troubled. Some of the heathen said the Christians were coming to steal their wives. Others declared the Christians were bewitching their people.
One day my mule had one of the worst spells he had
ever had, and almost killed me. We were attacked
from every side, but God witnessed that He was direct-
ing the battle, so we pressed on. Fear and curiosity
brought the people out to the few meetings we had in
the church building. God taught us some wonderful
lessons and gave us one hundred and fifty-three souls.
Many of these are still faithful servants of the Lord
Jesus Christ. A Preachers' Convention began on our
station the day our meeting closed. The students, rejoicing in the great victories they had won, marched
around the church building singing, "Forward into
battle, ye mighty hosts of God." Then they came inside singing, shouting and testifying to what God had
done in answer to their feeble prayers. The preachers
were so touched and blessed that they promised God
they would go back to their places of service to do as

the church at Endingeni had done. Several hundred souls were converted during that one effort.

g) Every One Win One.

Every Christian was to pray and ask God to show him some soul that might be won during the coming revival. It was very strange to see the ones the Lord laid on people's hearts: some were hard and disinterested, some lived far from the mission station. When we had all found the ones we were going to attempt to win, we visited them weekly. For some weeks the attention and prayers of each Christian were centered on the special friend he or she had chosen. On the big Sunday of the revival, every preparation was made for the guests. Dozens of little pots and pans were rounded full of carefully prepared food—the best that each could find. Most of the Christians went to accompany their friends to the service, and sat by their side to make them feel comfortable and wanted. God tendered many hearts, and gave us in that weekend meeting a greater harvest than we had even hoped to reap.

h) Meeting for the Heathen.

One time I asked our heathen friends if they would like for us to make a great big meeting for them alone. They said they would, and promised to come, if we would really make it for them only. We told them we would sing for them, pray for them, preach to them, testify for them, keep the altars open for them only, and that we would feed and entertain them, if they would come regularly. They seemed very happy and assured us they would be there. I sent out word to the more than fifteen hundred Christians of the district, telling them what we had planned, and asking them to bring their heathen friends. We told them that our whole attention would be given to the unsaved, that Christians would not be invited to the altars, that we would have no time during this period to help pro-·fessing Christians, and that if Christians came up to the station they would came to serve. We told the Christians that they might not even find room to get into the church services, that they might not get any food, and that they might not have any comfortable place to sleep. Of course everybody wanted to see the results of such an effort, so hundreds came in to help. We had weeded gardens for some of the chiefs, and were given two oxen for the work. I bought two more fat oxen. Every church sent a sack of corn. We dug many sacks of sweet potatoes, and made a few sacks of hominy. When the day for the meeting came, we rang the big bell early in the morning. But our hearts were sad, for it was pouring down rain in torrents. Many Christians and a few heathen had come in the day before. They had made a grass shelter over the big vat in which the meal was to be cooked, and with difficulty they cooked the big pots of meat which we were afraid the guests would not come in the rain to eat. At eleven o'clock we rang the bell again, and here the people came up every trail—men, women and children came holding their wet animal skins and blankets about them. There were several hundred of them. We put them in the center and front of the church where they sat huddled together on the grass covered floor of the big tabernacle. The rain continued, but they came faithfully every day. We dished up their food in big pans, wash tubs, wheelbarrows, big pieces of flat iron, and everything we could find. They squatted on the ground in age groups—men and women in separate places—and in spite of the dampness, they enjoyed themselves immensely. Had it been dry, they might have gone elsewhere to drink beer or they might have danced and fought on the mission station. So we saw that the rain was a blessing in disguise. God showed Himself in a wonderful way. During the song services, the people swung their bodies and sang lustily. At times the Spirit of God swept over us mightily. Sometimes the people would bury their faces in the grass on the floor, and wail as they prayed. I shall never forget those wonderful scenes. In one service alone over a score of these precious souls found Christ. Some of them were people for whom we had been praying for years.

The meeting was such a success that I often used this method to work among the unsaved, and every time they responded heartily. Recently others of our missionaries have tried this plan with good results. In a recent meeting, Mary Cooper of Gazaland reported several score of happy finders in one single meeting that cost only twenty-five dollars.

II. Medical Missions

1. *The Need of Medical Missions*

Show me thy faith without thy works, and I will show thee my faith by my works (James 2:18).

Africa is a land of disease. We cannot say to the African, "Leave your medicine men and your spirit worship," and then give them no help in their sickness. Every year multiplied thousands die for the want of the simplest kind of medical attention. Modern medicine is one of the greatest factors in breaking fetishism and releasing the soul of the African from bondage. God has especially worked through this method to gather in hundreds of converts, and to establish the baby church among our African followers. Field Marshal Smuts says, "The true ruler of today is the medicine man; and the only man to fight him effectively is the scientific medicine man. It is a matter for congratulation that our Christian missions are more and more developing their medical side. Medical missions is the mission for Africa." We thank God for our fine hospital at Bremersdorp with our God-sent doctors and nurses, and for our many dispensaries where yearly many thousands find healing for both soul and body.

In the Bushveld

It is midnight in the bushveld. In a little hut to our right a young man lies on his mat on the floor with a burning malarial fever. By the side of the sufferer an old woman beats on a drum made of a hollow log with a piece of deerhide over the opening. Early in the evening we begged a place to stay overnight, and all this time the old woman has persevered faithfully in her task. Other women chant and sing about the sick bed. We sit in a dark hut and pray. They believe a spell has been cast over the sick one. The people are afraid. They have no time now to listen to our message, and they have no confidence in our medicine.

We hear the tom-tom of the demon drum in a kraal near by. We crawl in at the little door. On the floor lies a woman in a trance. They say she is demon-possessed. We watch for hours, but we can see no twitch of a muscle or any sign of life. They say this woman has great power as a demon doctor, but that she has displeased the spirits, as she was thinking of becoming a Christian. Finally she stirs. Vile words pour forth from her lips. The circle of people clap their hands and sing wildly.

A loud cry pierces the blackness of the African night. Then there is another cry, and still another until there is a great wail of voices all about us. We run out from the hut to ask the evangelist what it means. We are told that the child of the chief has been very ill of pneumonia, and that these cries mean that the child has died. Everyone must show much grief, because tomorrow the diviner will be called, and someone will be *smelled* out as the one who hated the chief and caused his child to die. Any lack of sorrow now may cause suspicion tomorrow.

On the way home we see an old man holding a very sick boy by the legs. The boy's head is hanging downward, and the man is shaking him violently. The man has given the boy medicine, and now he must cause the boy to vomit. The process may be the cause of the boy's death, but this is the only way the man knows to doctor this kind of sickness.

We pass a kraal, and are asked to look into a cook hut. They remove several small logs and a grass covering from the door, and I crawl in to see on the floor a woman very close to death. Her body is yellow, and she has not spoken a word in several days. The people have never seen a sickness like this before, and they have shut the woman in the hut to die amidst the terrible stench. They think somebody has taken away the woman's spirit, and that something else is living in her body. Earlier this woman could easily have been saved with a few injections.

Here is another woman dying of a white man's disease. I have never seen a human being so nearly decomposed and still alive. I saw her reach her hand into a gaping hole in her thigh and pull out a handful of what had one time been flesh, while the dark blood oozed out over the naked limb. The woman died of hemorrhage a few days later.

Word came that Malingozi's sister wanted to be saved. She had a badly injured arm which had now become gangrenous. She took a hatchet when nobody was around, and tried to sever her arm from her body. A passer-by, seeing her plight, helped her finish the operation so she could live until the Christians came to help her find God.

Such suffering and fear may be seen any day down in the bushveld.

2. *Meet the Witch Doctor*

I went one afternoon to visit a friend. He had worked in the gold mines, and was now in the last stages of tuberculosis. He lay on his mat inside the grass enclosure that surrounded his little hut. I sat by his head on a low soap box. In a few minutes I saw through the opening in the fence two big, portly men coming toward the kraal. I recognized one as a diviner of our neighborhood. I taught his son in school. He was very friendly, and had tried to show me with his little pouch full of bones and teeth, how he *smelled* out the sorcerers that troubled his people. The other man, they told me later, was a very honored and famous witch doctor, old Mafuta (Fatty) from the bushveld. The people thought some witch had cast her spell over the sick man, but in spite of all they did, he continually grew worse. So they had called Mafuta to use his great skill in behalf of the sufferer. The two doctors stopped in the path. The diviner began to talk earnestly, and with many gesticulations, to Mafuta. He seemed to be trying to convince him to do something he was loath to try. In the end, Mafuta plunged through the opening in the fence like an enraged animal. With a blood-curdling cry, he leaped into the air, threw himself in circles, and waved over his head a long black horse tail. A beautiful leopard

skin was draped around his waist. His neck, arms and
knees were encircled with white cow tails. His head
was crowned with long *sakabula* feathers. Over his
body hung horns, pouches and little gourds full of
medicine. Skins, tails, horns, pouches and gourds
made an interesting sight as this huge man twirled
round and round in his screaming and leaping. The
native girls who had come with me almost tore the
fence down in their hasty retreat. They ran for home
with their hands crossed on their heads, screaming,
"Maye, Babo, Maye, Babo!" Presently Mafuta stopped,
stood at attention before me, smiled and said kindly,
"Sakubona, Nkosazana" (We see you, Daughter of
the King). If you were about to die, how would you
like to have your doctor make his entrance in this
manner when he came to visit you?

3. *Pulling Teeth*

When I went to Africa in 1920 it was necessary for
a missionary to do many things for people that are
done only by experts in more favored lands. One thing
every missionary had to do was to extract teeth. Since
filling teeth is entirely out of the question, there remains only one thing to do with an ailing tooth, and
that is to get rid of it. Certain native men can get
teeth out. But the crudeness of their methods cause
people to postpone calling on them as long as possible.
The method in brief is to take an instrument very
much like the farmers of the Northwest use in sewing their wheat sacks, and with this the gum is cut
away from the tooth, and the instrument is gouged

down beneath the tooth, and the tooth is pried out. Sometimes the operation is a long one, and the patient is so unruly that three or four persons must hold him down while the doctor gets the tooth. Often the injury inflicted is more or less permanent. To people accustomed to such procedure, the inexperienced missionary with his forceps is an accomplished surgeon. The native can scarcely believe the tooth is out, when the missionary does it so quickly. And although no drugs are used, the thankful patient almost always exclaims, "Why, is it really out?"

I had seen the methods used by my father and our neighbors in my girlhood days in our rural section of the state of Washington, and it was easy for me to sympathize with the natives of Africa. Also, having seen with what effort my father and our neighbors got their teeth out, I was exceedingly reluctant to try my hand at the business. So for some months after arriving on the field I managed to dodge tooth-pulling. Brother Shirley or some native helper was usually close at hand, and I always insisted that they do this work. But there came a day when no such helper was on the station, and a man came to have his tooth extracted. I went into our little improvised medicine closet to get the forceps, and to prepare a wash for use after the tooth was removed. I found myself trembling and wondering if I could really pull a tooth. In the medicine closet I prayed most earnestly that God would help me, and I came out somewhat assured, but still quite anxious.

The man and his wife had taken seats on the grass in front of the mission house. When I approached, the man said, "My wife also has a tooth she wants out, and she will have hers out first." It turned out that the woman had two teeth to be extracted. But her mouth was affected with pyorrhea, and I found no difficulty at all in getting her teeth. In fact they were so loose that they came out almost without effort. The woman was greatly pleased, and thanked and praised me most sincerely. The man's teeth likewise were diseased, and he had two taken out. This first success heartened me, and thereafter I never troubled to call anyone when there were teeth to be pulled. During my twenty years in Africa I pulled hundreds, I judge it would be no exaggeration to say thousands, of teeth. The patient sits on the ground, hangs on to the grass and opens his mouth, while we perform our "painless dentistry." My experiences along this line are just the ordinary experiences of the missionary in Africa, and I presume the experiences of the missionary anywhere that modern dentistry has not yet appeared.

4. *Spook Breaks*

Some of our Christians came one day and said, "There is trouble down at Chief Vlakazi's kraal. His favorite wife has had a terrible thing happen to her. Her face is broken. They say the spooks did it. The witch doctors have been called, and if something is not done, someone may have to die. And we think it will be Joseph's mother, for she is the one next beloved among the chief's wives. If you can do anything, please do it." Joseph was one of our Christian boys, and his mother was also very friendly to the Christians, and the thought that she might be driven away as the witch that had broken the face of the chief's favorite wife was indeed a serious matter.

I sent word to the chief that if he would bring his wife up to the mission station I would see if I could do anything to help her, but he replied to the messengers I sent, "Does that white woman think she knows more than our witch doctors? Even they can't cure a broken face which the spooks have slapped." So he did not bring his wife.

The woman's own story was that she was hoeing in the garden. Being a little tired, she leaned on her hoe to rest. Over in the near-by bushes, she heard a rustle, and then the spook jumped out and slapped her on the cheek and broke her face. And thus she was not only physically defaced, but she was the subject of the attack of spirits. She was bound to lose her place as the chief's favorite wife, and also whoever was found to be the witch by means of *smelling out* by the witch doctor would be severely punished.

What really happened, as the white man would put it, was that the woman stopped to rest a little, leaning on her hoe. The breeze rustled the bushes, and as the woman yawned as a result of the cooling affect of the breeze, her jaw slipped out of place. And knowing no way to replace the jaw, the poor woman was left disfigured and in pain and in trouble.

A day or two after our first information of the matter, our native Christians came again to urge that I go down to Chief Vlakazi's kraal to see if I could do something. So I saddled my mule, Coffee, and took along my little medicine case and the medical book that I had, and went over to the chief's kraal. I was not sure I could replace the jaw. I had never done anything of the kind, and had never seen a doctor do it, but I had read about it in the medical books, and it did not sound like too difficult a task.

When I approached the kraal, I found the women huddled in fear and trembling. All work about the place had ceased. The chief and the men of the kraal were out with the witch doctor preparing for the ordeal of *smelling out the witch* to find out who was responsible for the spooks' invasion of the chief's family. The belief was that unless the witch was found and the matter stopped, trouble would go right on through the kraal, and sickness, crop failure and even death to the members of the family might result.

I inquired of the women about the woman who was sick, and they merely pointed to the hut in which she sat. I got down on my hands and knees and entered through the low door. After waiting a moment for my eyes to become adjusted to the semidarkness of the windowless hut, I saw the woman sitting on the ground with her head and face covered with a greasy black rag. I asked about her trouble, and she tried, under the handicap of a dislocated jaw, to tell me the story of her work in the garden, and the slap from the spook. I approached her saying I might be able to help her, and that I would take a look. I placed a whisp of cotton around each thumb, as the medical book said to do, put my thumbs on her back molars, pressed down hard, and shoved the jaw backward at the same time. Much to my surprise, and to that of the native woman, the jaw slipped right back into place. The woman was jubilant with thanks and praise. The women of the kraal came to observe and to praise, and the shadow lifted from the chief's kraal. I explained to those who gathered about that if they practiced, they could do the same thing I had done.

My fame as a bone fixer spread, and pretty soon I found myself faced with impossible cases of dislocation—some cases being of long standing. Nevertheless, I was able to help some, and I think the whole matter was used for "the furtherance of the gospel."

Some time after this, in our camp meeting at Endingeni, the meetings being in charge of our native evangelists, and the crowd being composed partly of our Christians and partly of friendly heathen, a man yawned in the meeting, and his jaw slipped out of place. Immediately there was great excitement among the heathen, and our evangelists were able only with great effort to keep the people from stampeding. The heathen were especially surprised that the spooks would come right in among the Christians and break the face of a man.

I was at the dispensary a few hundred yards away. The evangelists assured the people that I would fix the man's face without delay. It was a serious and amusing sight to see a crowd of the brethren come leading and accompanying this man who had the trouble. In great earnestness, they said, "O Daughter of the King, you must do something right away or our meeting will be ruined." It was easy for me, on account of previous experiences, to put the man's jaw back into place. I then put on a little strip of bandage to indicate that I had done something for him. The company returned to the tabernacle and presented the man with his face restored, and the meeting went on with interest and victory.

5. *Witch Babies.*

Most Africans regard the appearance of twins or triplets a most unfortunate event. They think they cannot be human, since two are born at one time. One rainy day some of our women found two little boys, a few hours old, and weighing less than four pounds each. The babies were in a hole in the veld. One had been strangled by its own mother, and the second born was almost dead from exposure. They brought the living one to me stiff with cold. They had tried to wash the little fellow in the cold stream, and had fed him cold, soft porridge to try to strengthen him. I worked for hours before the little one began to show signs of life. We named him Tolakele (Picked-up-one). He lived several months, but never developed properly. He looked like a cute, little, old man. Most twins in Africa do not live to grow up.

Then there are certain babies that are supposed to be possessed with evil spirits. I remember one fine little baby that cut its teeth in an order not customary. It had to be sent away from the home where it would not bring a curse on other members of the family. Often these children never come back.

Many people fear that their children may be harmed by jealous people or that they may become sick from bewitchment, and so they hide them out in other homes, and often make them ill from improper treatment in trying to keep them from the witches. It is not uncommon at all to receive a little girl or boy as a gift from some chief or big man. They want to be friendly, but most of all they hope their child will be safely hidden, and have an opportunity to grow up. It is hard to refuse these children, and it is expensive to keep them. I usually accepted them, and then told the parents to keep them for me until they could go to school. This was generally satisfactory, since in this case the child was not theirs any longer. When the child entered school, and lived on the mission station, the parents would help with the expense. We got many converts from homes from which these children came.

Many women die in the kraals in childbirth, and leave their little ones motherless. Scarcely any of these children live.

On nearly every mission station we raise the neighborhood twins, the motherless babies, and the so-called witch babies. Then there are the sick babies, and those which are homeless for various reasons. The cute little black babies were always my delight. We kept them in soap boxes covered with white muslin on top of long white tables. I challenge anyone to find sweeter babies than the kind we have out there.

Our Christian natives have lately built a home for babies like these. We often speak of them all as "witch babies." We are expecting that we shall be able to save a great many more babies now than in former years.

6. *Little Bottles*

A little girl came to me for medicine for her mother who was very ill of malaria. I gave her calomel, epsom salts, aspirin, and enough quinine for several days. I had only powdered quinine, so I put it into capsules and explained over and over again just how to administer it. I was afraid the child might get confused with the different kinds of medicine, but she assured me she understood perfectly, and she ran off singing. The next day the child came with something wrapped carefully in a clean paper. She said, "I gave her the medicine last night and she is much better. Here they are, all your little bottles, Daughter of the King." I could not remember giving her any little bottles, but I took the package, and thanked her, rejoicing with her that the medicine had so quickly helped the suffering one. When in the house I opened the package, there were all the empty capsules. She had emptied out the bitter quinine, mixed it with all the other

medicine, and given it to her mother all in one huge
dose.

7. *Supplying National Workers*

We first contacted many of our workers through
our medical department. After the medicine man
had been unable to cure them, they were brought to
the missionary to see what he could do. Some of these
that I observed were:

a) Magodi-Norman.

Norman was a little herdboy who lived in a near-
by kraal. His father would not let the Christians
preach to his people. One day an angry cow trampled
Magodi, tearing his mouth and face very badly with
her hoofs. He became terribly infected. When they
could do no more for him in the kraal, they put a cloth
over his face, and brought him to the mission. He was
in such a terrible condition that the big flies followed
along in great numbers. It was not long until, by God's
help, little Magodi was well on his way to recovery.
He was not allowed to go home, lest the enemy who
had begun his downfall find him and finish him completely. He was a bright boy. God called him to
preach and to teach. He went to Natal, got a teacher's
certificate, and is now one of our most successful
preacher-teachers.

b) Mgwingi-Rodger.

Mgwingi, too, was a little herdboy. One day he
saw some lovely, ripe fruit on a high limb. He climbed
to eat his lunch. The brittle limb broke, and Mgwingi

fell on a sharp snag that tore a great hole in his abdomen, so that his intestines protruded. He lay for hours under the tree until at last he was found by his old father. After a few days doctoring with a medicine man, the child was given up to die. Willie, one of our schoolboys, found him, and led him to the Lord. After this, Willie walked daily before and after school the seven or eight miles to Mgwingi's home, expecting each time to find the little lad gone to be with Jesus. When the child did not die, I went with Willie one day to see if I could do anything, because the Lord had talked to me about Mgwingi in the night time. As I rode near to the kraal, I could smell a most terrible odor. They had pulled the boy outside, where he lay in the sun. The flies had been doing their worst, and the child was crawling with maggots. I felt that he could not live long, but I asked the father if I might take the child home with me. The old father said, "I couldn't refuse to let you take a corpse to bury." We went home, and sent boys with an improvised stretcher to bring the boy to the mission station. I cleaned him up the best I could. Brother Schmelzenbach had gone to Bremersdorp to try to get help from the doctor. But Dr. Hynd had patients he could not leave. Miss Carpenter came back with Brother Schmelzenbach to spend a few days resting at our station. I was terribly disappointed, but kept thinking all the evening and night about the Great Physician. I felt that we must try to save the lad, and that God's strength would take hold where our knowledge failed. Miss Carpenter was a good nurse. We persuaded her to help. We put Mgwingi on the girls' dining table. Brother Schmelzenbach and Willie prayed in the room while everybody else prayed outside. God heard and worked for us, after we had done our best. Willie and I took turns staying with Mgwingi every minute for several weeks. One night Mgwingi told me that when he got well he was not going back to his home because God had told him he was to be a preacher when he grew to be a man. In spite of many hindrances and testings, Mgwingi, now Rodger, has stood true to God, and lives with his little family in the bushveld. His missionary in charge says he is a most successful pastor, and that he has unusual influence with the unsaved.

c) Tatakile.

The medicine man cut a deep gash in Tatakile's forehead. They said she had too much blood, and some should be taken away. But the medicine man could not stop the bleeding, so he put pressure on the artery, and bound the head tightly with a black rag. Many times the blood would gush out freely, and they would bind the head again. After a time the wound became badly infected. Through sickness and loss of blood, Tatakile became skin and bones. One day her heathen mother appeared at my kitchen door. On her back Tatakile was strapped. The mother had carried the child eight miles from the bushveld. The child's pussy head was tied tightly with grass and a dirty sack. The mother tenderly laid the eleven-year-old girl before the door, and said she was giving her child that day into the hands of God. I cared for her, and soon she was normal and healthy. She took teacher training for the bush schools, and has for many years worked faithfully with boys and girls, leading many of them to God.

8. *I'm So Glad You Came*

Mcatulwane's mother was very ill, they said. I took a little bag of medicine and went over the hill to her kraal. The place seemed deserted, but when I called, a pitiful little voice answered, *"Ngene"* (enter). Inside the dark little hut I saw one of the most pitiful sights I have ever witnessed. A large forked limb of a tree lay on the floor. Hanging there in the limb was the wasted form of a little woman. When I asked in amazement why she was perched up there, she asked me to move her slightly to relieve the pressure on certain parts of her body. She told me she could no longer lie on her mat because of sores all over her body, and that Mcatulane had cut the limb for her, and before he went to work of mornings, he placed her on the limb, trying to put pressure on places that were not yet open sores. She was covered with bed sores all over her body, for she had been sick a long time and was unable to care for herself. The hut was dirty and foul smelling. At the woman's head was a tin can containing drinking water, and a little clay dish full of untouched porridge. The woman assured me she was not hungry, and that her boy loved her tenderly, and had done all he could to make her comfortable before he left for his day's work. While I tried to talk with her about herself and her need, she took my hand and kissed it and said over and over again, "I'm so glad you came." She said she had long wished that we would come to see her. Her Swazi friends, she said, were afraid to come, now, since such great evil had befallen her. She was hungry for God, and soon gave her heart to Him. I went to get a stretcher to carry her to the dispensary where we could make her few remaining days more pleasant. But the excitement of seeing a friend was too much for her. She had not been a Christian more than ten minutes, and I had not gone more than a quarter of a mile, Ntatulane said, until this woman went to be with Jesus. Whenever I think of medical missions or see parcels and supplies being sent to Africa for this most needy cause, I seem to feel again this woman's kisses on my hand, and hear her say again, in her dying words, "I'm so glad you came, so glad you came, Daughter of the King." There are many, many waiting that will be glad when the medical missionary and the supplies that God's people send come in time to help them find God.

9. New Projects

One of the new projects for the quadrennium—1944-1948—is to build a string of dispensaries down through the bushveld. These dispensaries will be built of stone, roofed with grass, and will each cost about $1,500. They will be near enough together that most sick folks will be able to reach one of them. Each place will be built near a native preacher's home where the

Christian native nurse will find friends and help.
These nurses will be girls who have finished their
training at our Raleigh Fitkin Memorial Hospital. The
government usually pays the salaries of these national
nurses, and the government is otherwise friendly and
helpful. The small thank offerings brought in by natives for examinations and for medicine buy most of
the supplies, so when the dispensaries are once built,
they are largely self-supporting. One of our doctors
will make a monthly visit to each dispensary. In this
way we shall be able to reach thousands of needy people. From this one project we shall be able to find
other national workers like Solomon, Marita and
Rodger, and should gather into our ranks hundreds of
children like Alfred and Hosea, and laymen like
Esther and Emely without number.

III. Educational Department

1. *Christian Schools*

When I first reached Africa in 1920, we had three
kinds of schools: the day schools, where children
spent a few hours daily, mostly with untrained teachers and very little equipment; the night schools, where
men, young and old, spent a few hours in the evenings
learning to read, write and cipher; and the Bible
School where young men were taught the Bible doctrines and Bible history, while they were also learning
to read and write.

Today we have scores of bush schools where
Christian teachers are giving hundreds of boys and

girls opportunity for primary education. Every main station has a school where children who have completed the sixth grade may finish the eighth and ninth years' work. At Bremersdorp we have a Teachers' Training and Practice School where girls who have finished Standard VII (first year high school) may take teacher's training for the bush schools. Our Bible School is at Stegi where we train our preachers and evangelists. We have hundreds of pupils in our church schools every week. The Sunday school in Africa is indeed the arm that reaches out into the darkness. Wherever the mission schools go, there is a great change in the neighborhood. In such communities one notices that the natives build larger houses and put in windows and doors. There will be homemade furniture in the homes. Often there are orchards of fruit, and gardens of vegetables. Sometimes they build their houses of brick, and irrigate their little garden plots. The boys have learned to do these things in school. You will find the houses clean, the walls decorated with clean, white mud, cornhusk mattresses on the beds, and little embroidered cloths on the tables and beds. If you stop in one of these houses, you may be served a nicely cooked chicken, and other native foods served in a very acceptable manner. You will love to see the mother as she spreads her clean mat on the floor, brings in her shining pans and clean clothes, and gives the baby his morning bath. There is nothing more remarkable than to see a neighborhood so changed in the space of a very few years.

The British government works with us in our mission schools. As soon as we get a school up to a required standard, we may apply for a subsidy for the teacher's salary. The government sends inspectors to all the schools to examine the work, and to help and encourage the teachers. From the fourth grade up the students take government examinations yearly. The government also supplies some equipment and machinery for certain schools, are always glad to advise, often furnish seed and young trees, and send agents to our schools to demonstrate new farming methods.

In all our schools much stress is laid on industrial work. Every school teaches the boys and girls to take the things at hand and exploit them for the benefit of the Swazi family. On all our main stations the girls are taught needlework, cooking, basketry, housewifery, gardening, etc. The boys have shops where they are taught carpentry, building and craft work. Since agriculture is practically the only industry of the native people, every main station has a good-sized farm. We teach our people how to rotate crops, fertilize and conserve the soil, plant orchards, and improve their stock. Thus equipped the people can buy their clothing, supply their other needs, and also have money for church offerings. All this serves to deliver our people from the temptation to brew beer to provide for their necessities. Then, too, from these farms we get nearly all the food used by the students—fruit, corn, beans, sweet potatoes, etc.

Our farming until now has been done in a very primitive manner, due to lack of machinery. We hope to soon have a light tractor on each of the five industrial farms of the main stations, and at least one truck in each of the three provinces in which our church is working.

2. *Where Is the Lord God of Endingeni?*

Sibande was sold to a heathen man, but she wanted to be a Christian. When she was almost grown, she ran away from home and came to the Girls' School at Endingeni (Schmelzenbach Memorial). She chose God and lived a Christian life, but she was powerless and undependable in her Christian service. She began to seek a clean heart. For months she sought, and then one night in family prayer Sibande (Elizabeth) was sanctified, and became an entirely different girl. Later she married John, one of our preacher boys, and they made their home at one of our outstations.

There was one church where the members were discouraged, and many had backslidden. The church building was leaning badly to one side, and was ready to fall down. The pastor's huts were old and leaky. I knew there were great possibilities in that place, and so I asked John and Elizabeth to go with their little family and try to save that church. After school I rode fifteen miles on muleback in the pouring rain to meet them at their new field of service. It was a gloomy day. We huddled around the little fire in the leaky cook hut, and moved about to keep from being drenched by the rain that came in rivulets through the roof. In the evening, we asked God to keep the church building from falling on the men who had to sleep there in order that I might stay with the women and children in the hut. Elizabeth was in poor health, and her children had colds. In the morning as I looked at the leaning church, the dilapidated huts, and the many discouraging things round about, I almost condemned myself for asking a man with a family to come to such a place to live.

We began to build. The natives for weeks carried stone by head and sledge for the walls of the church. We dug sand from the river banks, and carried it up to plaster the walls. They also began to build a home for their pastor. It was a long, hard job. At times when they were about to get discouraged and give up, I would go over and work a few days with them. One day we were plastering the walls of the parsonage with mud. I took the old women and the children and raced the girls and women and beat them. We were mud from head to foot, but the experience proved to be the tonic they needed. The quitting men came back to finish the roofs. In two days we did more than they would have done in their discouragement in two weeks.

Now a year had passed since John and Elizabeth went to Evusweni. I again rode the fifteen miles on muleback. It was a beautiful afternoon. When I came around the curve I saw a nice stone church, neatly pointed with cement, and roofed with corrugated iron. Around the yard was a fence of white

stones. The fence continued on either side of the
path down to the pastor's house. The parsonage was
a two-room mud house with a cluster of neat huts in
back. Flowers bloomed along the pathway. The house
was pretty with its homemade furniture, beds, tables,
trunks and chairs. Everything was spotlessly clean.
Pretty pictures hung on the whitewashed walls, and
embroidered unbleached muslin decorated the beds
and tables. A simple meal was on the table waiting
for the missionary. The next morning the church was
so full of Sunday-school children that some of the
classes were taken outside. There was a great crowd
for the morning service, with many friendly heathen
attending. The people sang and shouted and gave a
liberal offering. There was much blessing upon the
meeting and some seekers at the altar. After church
I looked at the day school register. There had never
been so many children in attendance. I walked down
by the river to see the nicely fenced school garden,
and the orchard that John had planted with government help and supervision. My heart swelled in
gratitude for the wonderful things that had been accomplished in one short year. I called Elizabeth aside
and told her how proud I was of her and John. When
I finished, Elizabeth said, "Daughter of the King,
would you like to know the secret of my part in this
success?" She said that one day when she was sick
and pressed, she came to the place where she felt she
could no longer go forward. Then she remembered
that at Endingeni while she was a student, God had

saved and sanctified her in answer to her heart cries. She was in school when we built the Girls' Home, prayed down revivals and got such marvelous answers to prayer. She reasoned thus: "God helped me there. Can't He help me here?" She said that mighty faith leaped up in her heart, and she grabbed her coat like Elisha of old, folded it up and beat the difficulties before her, shouting, "Where is the Lord God of Endingeni?" She said the waters parted and she found that God would hear her prayer out there alone just as He heard her when she was in school with many to help.

3. *From Bush School to Heaven.*

Marita loved much. She would go as a teacher to any bushveld school, no matter how dangerous the climate or how poor the pay. For years she received $1.75 per month for her hard labors over bright little Swazi boys and girls. One year it rained much. Her hut was very damp. She had malaria fever, and in her run-down condition contracted tuberculosis. For months she was tenderly nursed in the big hospital. But as the time drew near for her to go to heaven, she asked to be brought back to the dispensary at Endingeni that she might spend her last days among her friends and loved ones. She was bright and cheerful, and talked much of heaven. On the day she left us, she was especially talkative. The girls gathered about her to say good-by. Her old heathen mother sat on the floor at the foot of the bed. She preached to her mother and begged her to give her heart to Christ, so that she could meet her again in heaven. She gave

away all her possessions, and told us how she wanted
to be buried. She called everybody and said good-by.
When Lillian in amazement asked her if she was not
afraid, she answered without hesitation, "Afraid of
what? I chose Christ long ago, and served Him that I
might be ready for this moment." She talked of loved
ones whom she expected to meet in heaven. Of a sudden she tried to sit up, laughed, waved her hand, and
said hoarsely, "Good-by, girls, good-by. I'm going."
She sank down, and in a few minutes had made the
crossing.

There was no wailing for the dead that day. The
girls said they would not weep, for Marita was not
dead, but had just gone away on a journey. Without
a tear they carried her wasted form in the homemade
box and put it in the grave, saying, "We shall see her
again." Death to an African is a terrible and mysteri-
ous enemy. Marita's victory over death made a lasting
impression that none who saw her will ever forget.

4. *Alfred Gets His Tricycle and Other Stories.*

Little Alfred heard in Sunday school that Jesus answers prayer. He saw Richard Mischke's tricycle, and
like any little boy, wished to have one for himself. He
asked his mother where people get tricycles. But she
did not know. Since his mother who knew about
everything did not know, he thought he had better
tell Jesus about his desire. That night after he finished
his regular prayer, he asked Jesus to send him a
tricycle with red wheels, "just like Richard's." In the
morning when he arose from his mat to ask Jesus to

help him to be a good boy, he reminded Jesus again of his tricycle. Every morning and every night he always finished his prayer with the words, "And, Jesus, please remember the tricycle with little red wheels." After a few months his mother was concerned, and wanted to know if she should not stop him from asking for something he could not have. We decided that he would probably forget after awhile. But Alfred did not forget. When his tricycle was slow in coming, one morning his mother was amazed to hear him pray over his little dish of porridge, "I thank you, Jesus, for the porridge. And, please, Jesus, remember the tricycle." This continued for quite awhile. He did not seem troubled or doubtful, but day by day, morning and evening, before his food, in the Sunday school, and wherever Alfred prayed, he finished by reminding Jesus of his tricycle.

One day a white friend, who was going to Johannesburg where they kept toys, heard Jesus whisper, "And don't forget Alfred's tricycle with the little red wheels." She did not forget. When the package came, we asked Alfred what he supposed was in the box. He replied, "My tricycle." He rode it all day long up and down the grounds. When friends asked where he got the tricycle, he said, "Jesus sent it to me." When they asked how Jesus got it to him, he said, "I don't know. It came in a little box. I think maybe Jesus opened the window and dropped it down." When he was told who sent the tricycle, he said, "Oh, yes, Jesus sent it by her."

The Sunday school has brought many little boys and girls to know Jesus. Once we sent two little boys twelve miles to Pigg's Peak to get our mail. There were a lot of heavy packages. They thought that since they were given the packages they must bring them home. After they had gone a couple of miles, laden like little donkeys, they found their burdens too heavy. They were afraid to hide the parcels, lest they be stolen. Either of them was afraid to stay alone with the parcels. One said, "There is just one thing: we will ask Jesus to send a truck." They put their parcels on the ground, and laid their whistles in the grass while they knelt to pray. Trucks did not often travel on that road, and white men did not often ask little black boys to ride. But this was a desperate case. One prayed. The other began his prayer. They heard the truck coming. They barely had time to stand up. They did not have time to get their toys. The truck stopped, and the white man asked if they wanted a lift with their parcels. They were brought right to the mission gate before dark. They had to arise very early in the morning to return for their toys, but the main thing was, they had learned that Jesus answers prayer.

In the camp meeting Sunday school rally, the children were taught the little chorus, "My cup's full and running over." They sang it with motions like rocking the baby to sleep, like grinding the meal, like milking cows, like cutting wood, and other activities. The chorus swept through the camp until everybody, young and old, Christian and unsaved, was singing and motioning the little chorus. When the meeting was over, people carried this chorus to their homes, and continued to sing, "My cup's running over." One day I was surprised to see a company of heathen young men dressed in their animal skins, cow tails and bird feathers, galloping along the road like horses, leaping into the air, holding high their knobkerries, and singing loudly in Zulu, "Running over, running over. My cup's full and running over. Since the Lord saved me, I'm happy as can be. My cup's full and running over."

PART THREE—INTERESTING INCIDENTS

1. *Life in a Hut*

In the pioneering days in Swaziland practically every missionary at one time or another lived in a hut. It is remarkable how many other occupants insist on sharing space in a building like that. During my first week in Africa I was nearly eaten alive by fleas. Moving before an approaching storm one day, there approached our kitchen door what appeared to be a black goat skin. It was a blanket of fleas. We poured boiling water and sheep dip on our guests, killing thousands, and there were still enough left to take possession of our house. But after being bitten enough, I finally became inoculated. But even after that, the hopping was still annoying.

There were ants—white, red and black; big and little. The white ants eat up the books, pictures and all things made of wood. During my first year at Sabie I often came home to find that the white ants had cemented my army cot to the floor, and piled up the earth about the place. One morning I found piles of wings and legs on my kitchen table. During the night the red ants and the whites had had a battle, and these were the remains. The wounded had been taken away. The red ants won, and after that they had charge at my place. One night I observed a strange odor in the kitchen hut—like the odor of a wild animal. I shut the door quickly and called the natives for help. The house was alive with black ants. In the morning we gave them battle, and swept them out in piles. But they had already devoured our supplies, including a nice roast chicken that had been left in the soap-box cupboard.

We were scarcely ever rid of honeybees. Our walls and roofs of grass or corrugated iron made perfect hiding places. Any day one was likely to find the place taken over by these flying, crawling, stinging creatures. They climbed into the beds and crawled into our boxes. One day I opened a drawer to get a handkerchief and plunged my hand into a wiggling mass of bees.

I have seen chicken lice move down the wall of the hut like a curtain. Sometimes they forced the humans to live outdoors. Once when I was out in the kraals for several days, my white cotton garments took on the appearance of salt and pepper, and two days of such torment made me feel ten years older.

Moths often dimmed our little kerosene lamps at night. Cockroaches visited us in the darkness. Jigger fleas occasionally made their nests under toenails and caused painful swelling. Scorpions, snakes, lizards, spiders, rats, mice and other living creatures used to try to keep us company in the huts.

One fall in Swaziland it rained for weeks—every day. Everything in the hut was wet and mildewed. A spring of water broke up through my antheap floor. I dug a little trench under the wall to let the water escape, and for several weeks had plenty of water to use without having to carry it in. One night Fairy and I sat at our little table eating supper. Lightning killed several donkeys just a few yards from us. Then a terrific wind stole the grass roof from our house. We looked up at the dark heavens, down at the dripping table and the dishes now filled with rain water, then we laughed—and ran.

2. Soap Box Stage

We bought soap boxes from the traders at twenty-five cents each, and with these made most of our furniture. We nailed them one on top of the other to make the ends for our clothes presses. A round pole across the top made a place to hang our clothes, the boxes at the ends made places for linens, shoes and hats. A curtain provided the covering. A soap box lying on its side, with four legs on the bottom and a rack on one side of the top, makes a washstand. You wrap the legs and top with white muslin, paint and curtain the box, and there you are. We made our kitchen tables and cupboards of soap boxes. Our office desks and files were made of soap boxes. Every

boy and girl in the home had a soap box with a hinged
lid for a trunk. Even after we moved out of huts we
still found much use for the good old soap box. In the
dispensary, for instance, a box draped with white muslin made a lovely baby bed, and a number of such beds
could be placed on one table; or, with legs, they made
good bedside cribs.

Travel in those days was very difficult. There were
few roads of any kind. We had no cars. The rivers were
not bridged. Usually we went horseback over the
crooked, native trails, and waded the rivers or forded
them on horseback.

In those soap box days we lived like soldiers. One
was considered weak if he talked of a furlough. I slept
on an army coat most of the time for the first eleven
years. When Brother and Sister Schmelzenbach came
to America, in 1928, they left Paul, a lad of eleven
with me. During a period of several months Paul and
I did not see another white person. I often spent weeks
alone with the Bantu. It did not bother me. I forgot
that my face was white.

3. *Learning Zulu*

I agree with that missionary to China who said
that in learning a foreign language, one needs: the
wisdom of Solomon, the tongue of Aaron, the patience
of Job and the years of Methuselah. I began on Zulu
the next morning after I arrived at the Sabie Station.
Long months I practiced on the strange clicks, pressing my tongue against my teeth and quickly with-
drawing it to make it click, curling my tongue and

making popping sounds in the roof of my mouth, clicking my tongue on my side teeth like a farmer driving his horse and gently hissing at the same time, gargling and rolling strange sounds in every part of my rebellious mouth. These strange sounds had to be harnessed in combination with one or more familiar sounds before one could make simple words and short sentences. I practiced six months every day on one word before the natives agreed I had it right. I talked Zulu day and night, and tried faithfully to preach in it. Then one day in the Preachers' Meeting God anointed me as I preached from the words, "He smote thrice and stayed . . . . thou shouldst have smitten five or six times (II Kings 13:18, 19). Missionaries were amazed at the boldness of one who made so many and such pitiful mistakes. But even recently some evangelists told me the Lord still feeds their souls from the words of that message. I studied Zulu daily for fifteen years, and felt that I was just beginning to appreciate its beauty.

Attempting to learn a foreign language takes all the sense of superiority out of one. I have seen strong men weep like women over Zulu. And one does not get away from the danger of mistakes. I told a little lad to *warm* some high-priced peas for supper. But I used the word for *burn,* and the lad obediently dumped them into the stove. I used the wrong word when I told the caretaker to break off the sprouts from our young tangerines, and she proceeded to cut our beautiful fruit trees to the ground. I told little Hosea

to pour water "on the roots" of my fine, heavily laden
tomato plants. She removed the earth with her little
hands and poured water on the exposed white roots.
The Africans think these faded, colorless people who
have come to live in their land are a queer lot.

4. *"My, Didn't It Rain!"*

The drouth was persistent. It was long past planting time. The men of the neighborhood collected a
silver piece (half crown) from every person in the
neighborhood who wanted rain. This money was a
gift to old Chief Mnisi who was said to be the keeper
of the rain medicine. Messengers took the sack of
silver coins to the kraal of the chief and said, "Greet-
ings, O Chief. What wrong have we done, Great One?
We are dead. Our country is spoiled. We do not have
water even to drink. Here is a very little something,
Chief. Help us, O Mnisi." The old man cast a gleam-
ing eye at the silver, told the messengers that the ancestral spirits of the tribe were displeased and had
withheld the rain, and that goats and cows and much
beer would be needed, and that when all was prepared, it would surely rain. In fact he told them to
prepare their seed and their hoes. I had not been in
the country long, and when some of our lately converted Christians wanted to know if they should pay
money along with the others for their share in the
rain, I assured them with many words that only God
could make it rain, and that they would see that old
Mnisi could do nothing about it. Then we heard that
the rain was to come on a certain Wednesday. That

was our prayer meeting day. The Christians gathered in the early afternoon, and I took time to explain once again that the continued drouth was proof that the old rainmaker had no power, but was just making himself rich with the gifts of the people. When we came out of the meeting an hour and a half later, dark clouds were rolling up from the east, lightning split the skies, thunder rumbled throughout the heavens, and the rain came down in torrents. I looked up toward Mnisi's grass huts on the mountain side and saw men dancing wildly in the pouring rain, while others dragged goats up the hillside to increase the fortune of the rainmaker. Didn't it rain, and didn't I learn to talk less!

5. *Snake Stories*

I had been in Africa only a few days. The boys were playing in the Sabie River. I stepped into the tall grass to call them. Right in front of me a long black snake lifted his head above my head, looked at me with his beady eyes, and ran out his little forked tongue at me. I had never seen such a long snake in my life, and it is difficult to say which was the more startled—the snake or I. I stood transfixed—doing without intention the best thing possible. Had I screamed or run that black mamba, whose bite is almost always fatal, would have become excited and have struck.

One night I sat down to drink a cup of tea. Hearing a movement under the table, I looked and found

the table leg, only a few inches from me, wound about
with snake from top to bottom.

I stepped into the door behind Alice, our kitchen
girl, who stood washing dishes. I saw what appeared
to be a rope hanging from the grass roof in front of
Alice. I saw it move, and screamed for Alice to run.
It was the type of snake that spits into people's eyes
and blinds them.

I saw one of our girls slipping up behind me with
a club, as I sat at my office desk. I turned to see what
she could be after. Not five feet behind me sat a snake
ready for battle. The girl threw the club to me, and
I killed the intruder.

I was ready to lie down for the night in a native
hut. The preacher's wife brought me some matches
and told me to be careful, for the hut was full of
snakes. They had killed two puff adders and a mamba
that very day. I thought about it awhile, then said
my prayers and went to sleep.

One night I heard something moving outside the
hut where I slept. In the morning the tracks indicated
that a huge python had completely circled the hut.

I was preaching in an outstation. There was a
small window behind the pulpit. In the midst of the
service, the people pointed and screamed, "Snake!
Snake!" A long mamba was entering the church by
the window. Through windows and doors we were out
of the building in no time. The snake took refuge in
a nearby hut, and we spent the rest of the afternoon
in killing him.

Philemon slept on the floor at his grandma's. A snake came out of his hole and crawled about the floor. Grandma heard the sound, and arose to make a light. The startled snake, in his haste, ran right into the sleeping child's mouth, and bit him inside the cheek. He must have thought the child's mouth was the hole through which he entered. Grandma ran with the child to the mission station, where God, in answer to prayer, healed the child.

Snakes curl up in the clay pots and take a nap. They lie stretched along the end of the wall, like walking canes. They hide in your mats. They curl up beside the path and wait for someone to step on them. One learns to look before he steps or before he touches anything, anywhere.

6. *Clever Baboons*

Several times I have spent hours watching the baboons. When the troop goes out to eat they station watchmen. These watchmen sit in trees, on stones or on top of elevations where they can see the approach of an enemy from afar. There are usually three or four on duty at the same time on the different sides of the troop. We would sneak up as carefully as possible. But by the time our heads came into view, the watchmen gave the signal—a sharp bark, and every baboon scampered for hiding. If a baby loitered, the mother paddled him until he squealed and ran. In a few seconds not a baboon could be seen, except that now and then one could see the bright eyes of the partly hidden watchmen. If we remained quiet, we would soon hear the all clear signal, and the troop would reappear to find and eat their food. Mothers would sometimes busy themselves delousing their young. They would hold the louse in the fingers, look at him hard, then put him in their mouths. I could not make out whether they ate the louse or merely cracked him between their teeth. If a young one grabbed a green fruit, the mother would catch him, forcefully remove the forbidden fruit from the little throat, then eat it herself. The minute we lifted our heads again the danger signal would sound and the whole process would be repeated. The natives say that if danger comes to the troop because of the carelessness of the watchman, the others tear him apart limb by limb in their anger. I never watched the baboons but that I felt an added responsibility, recalling the words, "Son of man, I have made thee a watchman."

7. *Meeting a Lion*

They tell us in Africa that when one meets a lion he must not run away, lest the lion become excited and kill him. One must not stand still and tremble, lest the lion become emboldened. The safe thing is to push right on as though the lion were not there.

One late afternoon I drove along a narrow road in the lion territory. Miss Ora Lovelace was with me, and two national preachers were in the back seat of the car. Down the middle of the road meeting us came a huge animal. Our first thought was that it was a cow. But soon we saw it was a lioness. She lashed her tail, foam dripped from her mouth, and her eyes glowed like coals of fire. There was no place to turn, and I remembered we were not supposed to stop. When but a few feet remained between us, I whispered to Miss Lovelace, "Shall I bump her?" But at the last moment, the old lioness turned aside and walked around us, passing so close that I could have patted her head and rolling her big yellow eyes at us. She went a few feet to the side of the road and crouched behind a big thorn bush. We heard the deer coming, driven by other lions, and stopped to see the hunt. The other lions drove the deer right to the spot where the lioness crouched. She sprang once into the air, then lay down in the tall grass, while the frightened deer stood trembling. Then picking out a nice fat buck, the lioness went after her. The deer ran to the back of our car and circled us. The lioness cut in ahead of the car, and in leaping after her prey, stretched out so gracefully in the air as to look almost like a flying animal, and all but grazed the radiator of our car. In the disturbance, she lost the game, and returned to the road behind us. We thought it time to move forward, and then discovered that an old lion and three almost grown cubs were coming to meet us from the other direction. The appearance of another car was welcome just at that moment. The lions walked in and out between the cars, lashing their tails and growling. If I were writing a story with a moral, I would say that lions often get in the way of the Christian, and it does not pay to run or stand and tremble.

The way to live and enjoy victory is to keep moving on.

8. *Tidbits*

Speaking of hats—The gray-haired preacher came to church wearing a new hat made of palm leaves. It was nicely made, but it was a woman's hat, and had a ribbon flower on the side. A young man touched the flower and smiled, but otherwise the old preacher got away with his hat all right.

Special wedding garment—A man working in the mines sent his young wife a slip having lace and embroidery. The wife came to the wedding feast wearing the new garment on the top of her dress so all could see the fancy trimmings. A new missionary was the only one who was especially impressed.

Tribal marks—Nearly every tribe has a special mark, so that one can tell to what tribe a person belongs. The Swazi, by a very painful process, makes a hole in his child's ear, and inserts a reed until the place heals. When a child does not listen to his elders, they say he acts as though he did not have his ears pierced. One tribe cuts off the top front teeth—they say any dog or pig can have long white teeth. Other tribes file the teeth into points or burn or cut their faces or bodies.

Improvised medical instruments — A little boy stuck his tongue into the small hole on the top of a tin lamp, and could not remove it. The suction drew his tongue deeper into the little lamp. Infection set in. The frightened parents took the boy to the police.

The police brought him to the dispensary. We had no instruments with which to take care of such an operation. Missionary Mischke took a pair of big tin snips, used in cutting iron roofing. We gave the boy ether. Brother Mischke cut the little lamp away from the swollen tongue with the huge instrument, and the patient recovered nicely.

Water bearers—The Swazies are good to cats. They have a story that says cats will bring water in a gourd to people in torment in the next world, so they are good to cats here.

Baptismal requirements—A candidate for baptism and church membership is stood up before everybody and asked if he pays his tithe, if he is faithful in bringing his offering, if he belongs to the missionary society, if he desires one wife only, and other such questions.

Ornaments—A safety pin makes a good earring for a heathen African.

Superior creation—man—The native man is master. His women folks serve him. The goods of the kraal are his. He lives in the best hut, eats the best food, and sits in a place reserved for him at the gate of the cattle kraal. He is dignified, hospitable and courteous. A guest is welcomed, fed and slept as a true friend. Woman is bought with so many cattle, and even the children are not hers. There are foods, acts, words and privileges that are denied to women, and a man is shamed for doing a woman's work. But men and women are alike in their fears of other-worldly things, of darkness, of death and of the unknown.

Receipt for a wedding cake—"Five pounds of flour, five pounds of sugar, 15 eggs, two cups of lard, juice of a lemon, milk enough. Put in medicine (baking powder), if you have it. This will make a cake large enough to bake in a dishpan. Pour icing over the cake, and decorate with licorice drops. Place a shoe, a ring or a bride and groom on top." I saw a cake made by this receipt, without medicine. It looked like a huge, delicious Tillamook cheese.

Spending a night in a kraal—I was forced to spend the night in a strange kraal—the home of a man and woman, both witch doctors. A crowd of people were gathered in the largest hut I have ever seen. They made my bed of ten new mats, one on top of the other. I lay down fully dressed, with my feet toward the fire in the center of the hut. The woman witch doctor lay next to me: and then all the women, heads to the wall, feet to the fire. The children came next, and then the men. The husband, who was the head of the home, with several of his chief men, stretched their bodies right in the doorway. This was to keep the witches or any other enemy from harming the honored guest. There were, perhaps, twenty-five of us, all told, who slept in the big round circle that night.

Expressions of love—"You are refreshing as a gourd of sour milk. Please forgive my broken, rotten English, lover, Cheerio."—Young man to his lady. "You have taken a needle and sewed up my mouth" —Girl to boy. "The thing that causes me to write, child, is that I am overcome by a sickness that no doctor can find or help. He could not see that this man is killed in his heart by love for a girl. I beg of you, child, lance the abscess which is in the depths of my heart. I know, child, that you are the only doctor that can help me now. Put salve in this wound, child. I am in terrible darkness, give me light. Hear my prayer before you"—A young man to one of my pretty girls, too young to marry.

Letters from a girl to a young man: First letter: "Harry, I hear that your heart is in pain, but I ask you to forgive me concerning all your talk. It is I, Ruth." Second letter, "Harry, I read your words. It is black to me. I cannot understand. All these words overcome me. I say it is better you look somewhere else. Forgive, friend. It is I, Ruth." Third letter: "Harry, I have no more words which I can say. I just say God help you in your work. May God bless you. I will pray for you every day. Where you carry burdens in the work of the Lord, I will carry also. Goodby, friend. It is I, Ruth." This last letter sealed the engagement. The young man responded with a letter of thanks, and sent the silk handkerchief for Ruth to wear on her head as a sign of her engagement.

Solomon says thanks for the gift of a blanket: "We are short of words to express completely what is in our hearts for what you did for us. We were about to die with coldness. Surely God will just thank for us. This is really good blankets enough for Europeans. You would wonder if you see a person sleeping being a bundle as if it is a small child where else a man with a long beard would appear. That is the cause of feeling cold. It is really funny to see people sleeping like that. We were like that. But since from today, I mean the day our blankets from you came we know we are kings. We have nothing to thank you with. We just accompanying you with prayers."

Gardening—A Swazi gardener has always to cope with pests. The stock borers, birds, earwigs and weevils feed upon his corn from sprout to bin. The cut-worms bite down his bean stocks or the beetles eat up his blossoms. His peanuts may be killed by drought, mildew or blight, or they may be dug out by donkeys or deer or stolen by monkeys. Flocks of birds reap his kaffir corn. One year a fuzzy worm got into our sweet potato patch. We had either to go hungry or dig out those worms. We gathered about ten gallons of worms daily for several days and saved our crop. One day I saw a small plowed plot covered with thousands of snake eggs. That same year, in one week, the girls killed 67 snakes in one patch of beans. We always have to fight plant lice, ants, scale, smut and certain kinds of worms on our citrus trees. One year our trees were visited by a strange beetle. They hung in huge bunches, like swarming bees, all over the limbs of the trees. They damaged the crop for that one year, but we never saw them again.

During the summer one has to be ready at any moment to fight the locusts. When a cloud of locusts is seen, everybody grabs a tin and a stick, runs up and down his garden beating the tin and screaming at the

top of his voice. This often causes the locusts to pass
by and make their meal on another man's garden.
But often they cannot be driven away. They fill every
tree, and cover the ground like a thick red carpet.
They often eat every green thing that is in sight. In
the early morning while the locusts are still too cold
to fly, the natives gather them by the sackful, take
them home, boil and dry them. Thus prepared they
will keep for many weeks, and, cooked, they taste like
smoked smelt.

9. *White Man versus Native Man*

A white man sat visiting with a group of native
men. They asked him what the white people think
of the native people. He answered, "We like you,
but we think you are rather like children." The old
men were astonished and greatly amused. When the
white man pressed them for explanation, they said,
"This is very strange, indeed, white man; for that is
exactly what we think and say about your people."
The native says that a man lies down at night on the
hard floor, with a wooden pillow under his head, and
sleeps soundly until break of day. Only spoiled or
sick children roll and toss on the floor until they are
given a soft animal skin and a wad of soft feathers.
Men eat when the sun is high; only children have to
be fed in the early morning. Men run long distances
without tiring. They can kill a snake with the first
blow, and slay an animal with the first spear thrust.
One who cannot do these things is only a boy. Men
sit in a circle for hours, never moving about, talking

or interrupting, listening to the witnesses in an *indaba* (native trial). When the witnesses have all been questioned and cross-questioned, the matter talked to a finish and the offender punished, the matter is not to be discussed any more. No matter what the man does in the future, this offense is buried. Weak women and children squirm, and cannot sit still. The white people, the natives say, often judge before they can prove their judgments, and sometimes after a matter is finished, they continue to talk about it; and if a second offense is committed, they bring up again the matter that was once properly buried.

The white man says the native is black and pug-nosed. The native thinks the white man looks washed out, half-baked, colorless and pointed nosed.

The white man says the native is slow to learn, and can't remember. You explain to him the difference between the dish towel, the dish cloth, the floor cloth and the little white cloth he hangs around his waist. But when you return to the kitchen you may find him washing the dishes with the floor cloth, or he may come to the dining room with the dish cloth about his waist. He may wipe his perspiring brow on the corner of the towel, and the next minute begin polishing the plates with the same cloth. If you say too much about this, when you are not present, you may be referred to as "Little Rags."

But, on the other hand, the native thinks the white man can't remember. He recalls what you once said, and you think you did not say it. Before you can actually deny saying it, another native explains what you said. If you still cannot remember, they will tell you where you were, who was with you, in what month it was, where the sun was in the heavens, how big the leaves were on the trees, who passed by while you were talking, what others said, and will quote you word for word. You begin to recall a little, and they say, "It is bad. White man not remember. He much forget."

The native cannot see that the picture is hung crooked on the wall, but the very first time a man walks across the room, he can describe that man's disposition, demonstrate his peculiarity of walk, and describe the wart that is just back of his ear.

I once looked into a pot full of meat soup, the top of which was swimming in deep worm fat. This was considered a very rare and good dish by the natives; but I could scarcely eat supper that night. We never get used to seeing the children roast the big fat green worms on sticks and eat them so heartily. A new missionary looked into a meat pot, saw the whole head of an ox with eyes looking at him, discovered pieces of hide, horns and intestines, and remarked that it was all there except the "moo." A fellow missionary said, "You'll find the moo, if you stir long enough." But you should have seen our girls when they first tried to clean a slimy fish for the missionaries. You should hear them talk about "rotten cabbage" (kraut). And when an American friend sent Fairy a little bottle of limburger cheese, we had to remove it from the kitchen before anyone would come back to cook for us.

One day we noticed that the schoolgirls who did our washing mixed the towels all together. We asked them to keep them separate. They said they would separate them at the river and bring them home in proper order. We were chagrined to find that they did this by the smell, and more so still to learn that some of the girls could tell by the smell who was in the room, without looking. Also we found that certain old women would not come into our nice new house because the odor made them ill. They were surprised to find that white people did not know the white man has an odor. When I asked what white people smell like, they named a certain cheap cloth in the trader's store. And that cloth is not like delicate perfume.

The native, like the white man, is just a human being, childish and manly, ignorant and wise, weak and strong, disappointing and promising. He is affectionate and religious. He has qualities of heart, mind and spirit more priceless to the world than all the wealth of Africa's fertile soil and famous mines. When we deal with most things pertaining to western civilization, the native is a child; but the minute we step off the well beaten road and meet him in his own hills and velds, he is the white man's servant, friend, adviser, counselor, provider and protector. No one was ever safer when making a journey through the interior, than when accompanied by a native friend, whether he be Christian or heathen.

10. *Foods*

I am fond of most African foods. There are many kinds of wild fruits, and there are greens made of various weeds that give the native a change from his regular diet of corn, beans, peanuts and sweet potatoes. Besides beef and goat's meat, there are various meat foods like ants and locusts. Once I was invited to taste a young man's lunch. When I looked into his pail I thought I was looking at a baby's skull. It turned out to be monkey meat, but it overcame me. I like the sour milk drinks. Ants and locusts are fair. I can live a short while on hard cornmeal porridge. But worm and monkey meat I did not taste.

A friend sent money to build a chapel. At the dedication, I was called to eat with the people. I was put alone into a hut filled with food. There were great dishpans full of all kinds of native foods, and an eight gallon clay pot full of sour milk. I could not eat all the food, so the people finished what was left. Then they gave me a big ox which they had earned by weeding the chief's gardens. This I was supposed to drive to the friend who had given money for the chapel. But since it was too far to drive an ox from Swaziland to California, I sold the animal and sent the money to the friend.

One time I was up in the mountains and very hungry—had had no food since daybreak, and we had climbed for hours up the steep mountain side. At sunset I heard a squawk. Half an hour later I was served a huge dish of hard porridge, and a whole chicken, plus a few small feathers and certain parts of the chicken which are not usually served. I was too tired to eat the hard porridge, and too weak to take the raw meat. When the food came back in the same form for breakfast the next morning, I cut it up and put it in my saddle bags, and later on traded it to little children for raw peanuts and boiled beans.

One day in my work I passed near a great chief's kraal where they were having a wedding feast. The chief sent men to urge me to come and eat. I could not afford to offend, and so turned in. The chief himself, not a servant, as might have been expected, brought the food to me. A large wooden dish, such as only members of the royal family use, with half of the head and chest of a huge ox, along with much soup was placed before me. The chief came crawling, and thus served me in the most respectful manner, while the people clapped their hands to help me thank him. He unfastened the big knife which hung from his side, cleaned the knife on the grass, and handed it to me. The women politely crowded about to watch me eat the warm, saltless meat. I chose portions of the tongue, and chewed in misery for a long enough time to show my appreciation. I decided I would not want any more tongue for a long time. My girls came to my rescue and finished the huge serving of meat and soup that had been my portion.

11. *Christmas Stories*

Christmas comes in midsummer in sunny Africa. Everywhere the people sing out, *"Kisimusi Bokisi, Nkosi"* (Christmas box, King). The mission always has some kind of celebration, and the native Christians try always to have oxen or goats and rice for the Christmas feast.

We try to give every native that lives on the station a little gift. A safety pin, a yard of cloth, a half cup of rock salt, a penny box of matches or a little piece of soap makes a fine gift for older persons. The children get a little bag of cheap candy—usually the only taste of candy they have during the year. We search for days through our boxes and trunks for anything we don't have to keep to give to the few hundred people. When parcels from America arrive, it is not so difficult.

One year our Christian children decided to invite the heathen children of the neighborhood to our place for Christmas—the Christian children to give their candy and gifts to the others. We made doughnuts, and stripped our plum trees of their fruit. We cut a big eucalyptus tree and decorated it with cotton, bright paper, popcorn and about a hundred toy balloons that some good friend had sent. That night we had about two hundred guests. We put all our lights in the tree, so the rest of the big building was not very light. The teeth and eyes of the black children gleamed in the dimness. It was the first Christmas celebration for most of our guests, and we could not keep them quiet.

They were like wild goats—pinching, jumping, yelling and laughing. Every child received a plum, a doughnut, a little bag of candy and a small gift. Many of the boys received one of the little balloons. These each promptly popped on his neighbor's head. Our Christian children rendered a nice program. But it did not seem to us the heathen children saw or heard. After the meeting, the girls went to bed with little trouble. We slept them on the floor in long rows, as we sleep the women and girls at camp meeting time. But the boys would not quiet down, making it impossible for anyone in their house to sleep. Before sunup, the children all went home to herd the cows and goats. We thought they had not heard our program of stories and songs. But we were mistaken. They described it all to their parents, and the parents were pleased. We made many friends. Some of those children are in our Sunday school now, and some of them are Christians.

12. *Spiritism and Magic*

To the African the rocks, rivers and trees of the veld are not sufficient to afford lodging for all the spirits. Spirits inhabit the whole material world: some live in homes, some wander about, some lodge in fallen trees, some possess men, some live in animals, some are easy to be propitiated, some are vile and open to the suggestions of evil people—servants of your enemies. Spirits bring sickness, accidents, floods, droughts, pests, death and all misfortunes. Your dearest friend may be a witch. The African may deny

himself certain foods, refrain from certain acts, refuse
himself the pleasure of keeping his own child (law of
taboo), hang his body with charms, observe all the
customs, pray and make offerings to the ancestral
spirits, and work tirelessly at it all, but it is all an ex-
periment. It may all fail him. A man who breaks a
taboo, even unconsciously, has no excuse for his ignorance: he does not prosper, evil befalls him or he
may sicken and die.

The Bantu say, "God, having created us, forgot us.
Man despised God, then God sent him away." Alone,
this created being must find some way among his
difficulties. He needs someone to make rain when
the heavens are dry; someone from whom to get the
charm; someone to tell him from what to abstain;
someone to mix the love potions; someone to doctor
the hoes, huts, gardens and graves. He needs medicine to compel the witch to take away the bewitchment. The helper he needs is found in the witch
doctor.

Matopi was a demon doctor. At the death of her
Christian son, she was converted, and for a time was
free of demon possession. She became ill, and as she
grew worse, heathen friends told her it was because
she had given her demon outfit to the missionaries, and
she must sacrifice a white goat, lest she be killed because of the possessions that had been carried across
the sea (they brought them to America). Alone, she
became afraid, and offered the goat. From that moment the demons took possession of her again. Hear-

ing of her plight, I called to find her lying on the ground, foaming at the mouth and roaring like an animal. Could this be our Matopi who had been so transformed and Christlike? She circled me on hands and knees, muttering and glaring, when we prepared to pray. While we prayed, she lay like a stone, but when we stopped she screamed, threatened and cursed. I asked if she knew Christ. In a strange and terrifying voice, she screamed out, "We know Him! We know Him!" Still circling us on hands and knees, she spit into the air, raved in the face of God, and cried, "We hate Him! We hate Him!" We prayed, and seemed to get some help. But under the influence of her four doctor friends, Matopi refused, and a few months later when in one of her demon spells went out into eternity.

13. *More About Zulu*

The whole structure of the Zulu language is governed by the noun through its prefix. This is the secret of the wonderfully regular construction of all the Bantu group of languages, differentiating them from European languages. The Bantu race is supposed to occupy the southern half of Africa. These people are supposed to have left their primal home over two thousand years ago, and to have migrated south and west. Their history is traced by their speech. His language with its idioms, proverbs, irony and richness of expression fits the Bantu like his skin. The Zulu speaking people are a part of the Bantu race.

a) Proverbs.

The Bantus enliven their language with thousands of proverbs which are in daily use. They say, "To see once is to see twice" (Once bitten, twice shy). "We will ask for the meat when it is cooked" (Wait and see how it turns out). "The eye crosses a full river" (Desire outstrips possibility). "I climbed up easily. The trouble is in getting down" (It is easier to get into trouble than to get out).

b) Words and phrases.

The Zulu tongue is much richer than ours in its copious supply of words which fall within the scope of the observations and necessities of uncivilized man. For instance, there are a dozen or more words which designate periods of time from midnight until sunup. There are: the big night(midnight), the very beginning of day, the first change of light, time of the morning star, the very first appearance of dawn, when the horns of the cattle can be discerned, at the crowing of the cock, at the descent of the fowls, very early in the morning, early morning before sunrise, at the dawning, at still dawning, at the coming of the sun, and others.

c) Word Pictures.

"Remember the rabbit." The African rock rabbit, like our "cotton tail," has a tail noticeable for its brevity. The natives have a story to the effect that when God made the animals, He made them somewhat piece at a time, and finished up with the tails. There came a day when all the animals were to come to an appointed place to each receive his tail. But the rock rabbit was busy or lazy, so he simply said to another animal, "You bring my tail for me." But this other animal forgot to ask for the tail for the rock rabbit, and ever since the rabbit has been tailless because he left to another what he should have done himself. Now when an African is about to delegate a personal responsibility to another, his friends warn him by saying, "Remember the rock rabbit."

"Everywhere the pot is three-legged." One of our boys went away from home to work, thinking it would be easier to be a Christian in another place. He imagined the world was more friendly, and the work more agreeable in other parts of the country. But after a few months, he wrote, saying, "You would be surprised, Teacher, it is three-legged everywhere." The Zulu proverb says, "It (the cooking pot) has three legs wherever you find it," meaning that things are about the same the world over.

14. *Interesting Names About Endingeni*

Pendukani—Pendukani (Repent ye) was the name of the first automobile ever used on our station. The car belonged to Brother Schmelzenbach, and he printed in big white letters on the cover of his spare tire this Zulu exhortation, "Repent ye for the kingdom of heaven is at hand," and the car came to be known as Pendukani.

Fairy and Louise—These twins were left motherless on the day of their birth, March 3, 1938. That week they became members of our big mission family. One was little, delicate and fairylike. The other was boyish, hungry and had strong lungs. Miss Carpenter, who was then our nurse, began to call them Fairy and Louise. I will leave it to you to decide which one was Fairy and which Louise.

Dulile—Nearly every missionary is given a native name. In the early days I talked a lot about expensive soap, books, etc., trying to teach the natives thrift. Then I preached a deep experience of grace, obtainable only by a great price. So the natives came to call me Dulile, a name that means deep, expensive, high-priced, and by that name I was known among both natives and whites. The girls made a song—a praise song, as their custom is, and sang out, "Do! Do! Dulile! Do straight! Do right! Do everything right!"

Coffee—Veteran Mule—We bought Coffee for sixteen pounds ($80). It required an expert to saddle him. Often he kicked the saddle high into the air several times before it could be secured on him. It was a problem to mount him, for both his teeth and his heels were dangerous. Once aboard one was usually all right. Once a dozen men worked at saddling him, while he tore down a fence and broke several trees, and then they gave up. I had to ride Coffee home that night. One time he was unusually docile for a week, eating from my hand, and putting his head and neck into the hut door to get his corn. I decided that naturally he was tame, but that the natives irritated him. Then without warning he turned on me, teeth gleaming and ears laid flat. I ran for the hut, Coffee after me, and just as I disappeared into the hut, he wheeled and kicked the door with both heels, and trampled a washpan until it was flat. But Coffee is an easy rider for a mule, is immune to horse sickness, can climb the hills and travel through the hot bushveld and lives on less food and water than is possible for a horse. In fact Endingeni would not seem like home without Coffee.

Crazy Lomdununo—We have no insane asylums in Swaziland, and only the very dangerous of the insane are sent away. Crazy Lomdununo was our nightmare. She was capable of doing anything. She burned down one kraal, ripped the door off another, tore a young kid in half with her hands, stole a baby from its mother and swung it back and forth by its feet, lived on food from anybody's garden, helped herself to any thing she desired and was a neighborhood bugaboo. A blood-curdling scream in the evening was announcement that Lomdununo had come to the mission station. One time she pulled up all our flowers, at another time it was our vegetable garden, and often in the dead of night we would hear Lomdununo trying to get into our house. She would climb into the house and hide behind the door. Then when we stepped into the dark room, she would leap and grab us. Sometimes she chased us with clubs and threw refuse on us. Once she just missed my head with a large stone. Everywhere she was feared and resented. One dark night in a little bushveld church, where we had only a small dim lantern for light, during the altar service, I heard a slight noise, and looked up to see Lomdununo's body wiggling through a high, small window, and before I could collect myself and prevent her purpose, she landed right in the midst of the seekers at the altar. She would come to the camp meeting every year, and always caused a scene, and sometimes trampled children in the crowded tabernacle.

One night just before I left Africa, we were eating supper very late. We had been talking about a man in the neighborhood who had been murdered to make medicine for witchcraft. The big curtain behind my chair moved. Fairy screamed, and there beneath that heavy curtain on the floor, flopping back and forth, was what seemed to be a bodiless human head. Lomdununo had heard that I was leaving, and had come to say good-by.

Part IV—Missionary Addresses

A. Bringing the King Out

In the year that King Uzziah died, I saw the Lord sitting upon a throne, high and lifted up (Isaiah 6:1).

During the month of December, the Swazi nation celebrates its Firstfruits Ceremony, the greatest ceremony of the year, called the *Incwala*. At the proper time, old Vanyana, the chief witch doctor, and certain of his men go to the kraal of the Queen Mother, and there, from a certain hut, bring out the calabash that is used to carry water from the ocean for making medicine. The men of this kraal quickly kill a black ox and make a covering for the calabash. This serves as a pad on which to carry the calabash, and also protects it from harm. They squeeze the gall bladder over the calabash, and return with it to the king's kraal. At the proper time, Vanyana starts on his pilgrimage to the Indian Ocean to fetch the sea-water. Just before sunrise the company go to the shore and and dip water to fill the calabash. After a ceremony on the shore, they start for home, but they do not hurry. Soon they turn in at a kraal of a chief or head man. The party loudly sing the praises of their king, while the head man hurries to kill a big, fat ox. This ox is not a sacrifice or a requirement. It is a free gift. Vanyana and his party eat the meat with the members of the household, and then take the tail and tie it to the side of the calabash. When they stop at the next kraal, all this is repeated, and the second tail is tied on the side of the calabash. At every kraal visited another tail is added to the collection of long, pretty ox tails hanging from the calabash.

Back in the royal kraal the king will see the ox tails and hear of the beasts that were slaughtered in the different kraals along the way. His heart will rejoice, and he will not forget these men who made such wonderful gifts to him. Often, if one wishes to see the king, he must spend weeks and sometimes many months before he can get audience. But if one of these come who has hung a cow tail on the calabash or any of his messengers, the wait will not be long.

The remembrance of that cow tail will bring many
favors from the king.

At sunset in the black of the moon, King Sobhuza,
Vanyana and several of the chief men go into a special
hut. The king will come out at the coming of the new
moon. Early in the morning of that day, dancing
commences. Nearly all of Swaziland is present, and
nobody does any work all day. The queen mother will
wear her most beautiful leopard skin cloak, and be
prominent in the dancing. The king's wives, wearing
bonnets made of baboon skin and decorated with a
special kind of iron beads, may be seen and admired
on that great day.

In Swaziland a well-rounded person is considered
beautiful, and the king's wives are often plump and
pleasing. The women have their hair piled high and
decorated with pretty colored mud. They will be
dressed in skins highly decorated with bright beads; in
their hands they will carry small looking glasses, and
they will take their part in the dancing. Even the
children, each dressed in his or her very best string or
skin or cloth, join in the fun. The warriors are the
most fascinating of all. Their headdress is made from
the beautiful feathers of the sakabula bird. Their
decorations are made of white cow tails worn in ring-
lets around neck, arms and ankles. Their covering is
of pretty leopard skins. They carry bright colored
shields, looking glasses, and on this day only a stick
in the hand.

All dance and sing and praise the king. They dance in front of the hut in which the king is closeted. They dance singly and in groups, and call out the praise names of their beloved leader. They all want him to come out so they can see him in their midst and be rejoiced by his presence. They surge forward and backward. When the king opens a little crack of the door and peeps out at them, they sing and dance more wildly than before. At last, satisfied with their praise, the king steps out, and every heart is thrilled by his presence. They feel that now everything will go well, and that no harm can befall them, since their king has come out into their midst.

As soon as the king appears, all the young men of the army take up their hoes, and accompanied by their king, go out and weed a field of corn. This is a token that they will hoe the gardens of the king and be faithful in his service wherever they are sent. One time I looked over the hill at a little kraal built in the corner where the lands of three chiefs met. I asked the old chief with whom I was talking to which one of the chiefs this Swazi belonged. He stoutly denied that he knew such a man, and pretended he could not see any Swazi man's kraal. In the end, he said, "Oh, Daughter of the King, you mean that wild dog down there. He isn't a Swazi." This man was born a Swazi, but he would not listen to the chiefs. He would not be sent by them or do any of the things Swazies are supposed to do. In other words, he would not hoe in the king's gardens.

Later in the ceremony, young men of certain stipulated qualifications, who have been properly prepared, lay aside their finery and come only in their loin cloths. A bull, every hair black, has been driven into a small inclosure at the top end of the cattle kraal. The king, who is with Vanyana at the top of the cattle kraal, takes a certain special stick and strikes the animal to infuriate it, and make it a match for the brave soldiers waiting outside. The gate is opened, and as the bull charges out, the king catches it by the tail and shouts, "Here he is, young men." The soldiers jump on the animal, catching it by horns, legs and tail. They pound it, pinch it, kick it, get it down on the ground and hold it while others put their hands over the nostrils to suffocate it. They must kill the bull with their bare hands.

When the whole ceremony is over, the people go back to their homes fortified against evil, and secure in their belief that they may now eat the fruits of their labors with gladness and safety.

At our recent General Assembly two great banners were hung in the front of the large auditorium. One gave us the Home Missionary goals, the other the Foreign Missionary goals for the quadrennium. Putting these goals all together, and analyzing them, we find that there are four principal objectives. These are: a million dollars a year for Foreign Missions, a thousand new churches during the quadrennium, two thousand new preachers and missionaries during the quadrennium and a million souls in two decades.

Looking more closely at these goals, we see that a
million dollars a year means five dollars a year for
each member for a lost and dying world. This counts
our General Budget, our native workers fund, our
medical missions money, and any special money that
may be given to take care of approved specials.

A thousand new churches during the quadrennium
mean just a little better than one new church a year
for each thousand members. Some districts have often
reached and surpassed this goal. We should have a
hundred Negro churches during this quadrennium,
since the policy is now drawn up and leaders appointed to direct this division of the work.

Two thousand new workers during the quadrennium—five hundred for the foreign field, and fifteen
hundred for the home work—means that out of every
hundred of our members, one is to prepare himself
as a Christian worker during the four-year period.

A million souls in two decades means merely a ten
per cent increase in our membership each year of the
period. We could not set easier goals and expect God
to pour out His best blessings upon us. We thank God
for leaders that gave us goals worthy of our great
Lord and Saviour. We thank God for the Church of
the Nazarene that now marches forward to reach these
objectives. I am glad God gave me the privilege of
being a Nazarene, and I mean to do my share toward
helping to reach the goals that have been set.

It will be easier for us to reach these goals than
any of us think, if we will just each one pray and do

his part. God does not need much to begin on. But
it will also be quite easy for us to fail, if we are even
just a little slow and careless. Battles can be lost for
the want of a horseshoe nail. Part of our time has already slipped from us. If we expect to succeed, there
are four things we must do:

First, we must get the King out. It is not enough
for us to proceed as we are. We must have a new view
of our King. God must give us our plans. God must
call the workers. God must lead us in the battle. God
must draw the people and convict them. We must
have much of God or we miserably fail. How shall
we get His presence among us? Just like the Swazi
people bring their king out from his hiding place. We
must desire Him, seek Him, follow after Him and wait
for Him until He comes. I do not know why God has
set such a premium on prayer. I do not know why the
great God of heaven should be moved by the petitions
of little people like us; but I know He is. When I speak
of prayers, I do not mean the halfhearted prayers that
we often pray morning and evening or on the run as
we go about our work. I mean prayer that will not be
denied, prayer that takes hold of the arm of God,
prayer that "laughs as impossibilities, and cries, 'It
shall be done'." I can illustrate the kind of prayer I
mean by an incident that happened in Swaziland.

We had asked God to give us twenty-five seekers
at our altar in the local church during the quarter.
We had also planned the first Mothers' Day celebration we had ever observed in the Girls' School. Many

of the girls' mothers were unsaved. Most of the unsaved ones had never outwardly forgiven their daughters for refusing to go to the men to whom they had
been sold. We had been praying much, asking God to
soften their hearts and send them up so we could
show them how much their children really did love
them. Our quarter was drawing to a close, and we
had had very few of the converts for which we had
been praying. As I kept bringing these two requests
before God in prayer, it seemed to me that He kept
asking why I did not request that these converts be
from among the mothers of the girls. I tried to put
the suggestion from me many times, for these women
seemed hardhearted and angry, and we did not even
know whether they would come to visit us. It seemed
too hard to ask or to believe. The impression grew
upon me, until I began to ask God seriously if it could
be His voice speaking in my heart. Presently I felt
sure that I was not mistaken. All the girls joined the
missionaries in praying that God would give us these
converts on Mothers' Day. Finally, when I realized
how utterly impossible it would be for this request to
be granted unless God did a very unusual thing for
us, and since it seemed that He was willing to do it, I
decided we might as well ask largely anything we
desired, for if He were going to come that far to help
us, we might just as well have anything we could ask
or think, so I took away all restrictions. I asked God
to do anything and everything God could do for these
mothers, and to show us how to prepare the way so

man would not restrict God. My faith grew more and
more as I prayed. Then God gave me this verse, "Thou
hast asked a hard thing: nevertheless, if thou see me
. . . . it shall be so" (II Kings 2:10). I immediately
thought of the Incwala. I remembered how the
Swazies pressed closer and closer and would not stop
or rest until they brought their king out to stand in
all his glory in the midst of his people. I said in my
heart, "We shall bring the King out." We began to
pray in earnest. We fasted and waited on God many
hours day and night. I shall never forget the last night
before the guests came in on Friday. We prayed until
after midnight. The Lord was so very near and precious. It seemed that He was just about to step out
into our midst. Finally, the girls were so blessed that
they walked up and down the aisles shouting and
praising God. Our burdens were gone. The Lord was
very, very near to every one of us. We went home to
get a little rest. Before I shut my eyes in sleep a sense
of disappointment and frustration crept into my heart.
A voice seemed to reproach me, saying, "He did not
come out." He had merely peeked out at us, and we
had been satisfied. Instead of pressing closer and
closer until He really came out into our midst, we had
come home to rest. I said, "It is not too late. We will
go back and wait until He does come out." We prayed
all Friday morning, everyone at his desk. Noon came,
and still Christ had not come out. In the early afternoon the time drew near when the guests should be
arriving. Everybody began to pray aloud. They

pressed in closer. It seemed that the wall now was very, very thin that separated us from our King. We praised Him, told Him how we loved Him, and that we must have Him. We begged Him to come out from His hiding and let us behold His glory, that we might be sure we had done everything we could to prepare His way. Of a sudden the wall seemed to fall down, and there stood King Jesus, high and lifted up. Somebody started the song, "There He stands the Mighty Conqueror, since He rent the veil in two." Great blessing and assurance flooded our hearts like mighty ocean billows. We knew that God would do all that God could do, since we had done all we could do. Wonderful things followed. The mothers came in. When we saw their numbers, Fairy came and whispered in my ear, "Do you still believe?" I said I did, and she answered, "If you still do, I do." We fed the mothers, sang to them and played with them. When they slept at night we were too excited to rest much, so we spent much time praising God and preparing for the next day. The girls circled the church in which the mothers were sleeping and serenaded them in the night time. We showed the mothers our work on Saturday, and played games most of the day. On Saturday night twelve girls sang in English, "The Ninety and Nine." Each child had a gift prepared to give to her mother as soon as the song was finished. The mothers did not understand a word of English. But as the girls sang, great tears rolled down their cheeks as they looked at their mothers whose souls they had been seeking so long. One woman jumped up, lifted her hand, and said, "I choose Christ." She said she could no longer contain herself, but must find rest for her soul. Another woman followed, and most of the others fell on their knees and buried their faces in the grass on the floor. Every child ran to his or her mother with his gift, and there was much sobbing all over the building.

At sunrise on Sunday morning we went to the church for an early morning service. God had given me a message, "Can a woman forget her sucking child, that she should not have compassion on the child of her womb? Yea, they may forget, yet will I not forget thee." So mightily did God manifest Himself in our midst that the two women who chose the Lord the evening before came to the altar and fifteen others followed. A wonderful work was done in every heart, and in after years, as a result of that weekend meeting still others found God. This is the kind of praying and believing we must do if we expect God to come out and help us reach the goals we have desired of Him.

In the second place, if we reach our objectives we must all hoe in the King's garden. We cannot leave it to the women of the Missionary Society to hoe alone. They will do their best, but they cannot finish the garden. The pastor must hoe. He will have to hoe as he plans and hoe as he preaches, he will have to hoe as he gathers in the money, and as he calls his young people to the altar to dedicate their lives to the service of the Master. He will have to hoe as he leads his people to help in establishing new churches, and in winning souls and getting them established in their Christian walk with God. But we cannot leave the hoeing for the preacher to do alone. All the men must hoe. Men's shoulders are broad and made for heavy burdens. When hoeing in the King's garden the men and women do the heaviest work. The young people finish up around the edges, and carry on when the others are tired. The old women and the children pull the weeds from around the tender plants with their hands. Everybody must hoe: the old people, the W.F.M.S., the pastor, the young people, the Sunday school, parents, little children, every individual in every church everywhere. There must be no "wild dogs" among us.

In the third place, we must not forget the cow tails on the calabash. You remember that the owner of the ox had already paid his taxes, and his ox was not a sacrifice. It was not required of him. It was a free gift. He was able to give it, and he gave because he delighted in his king. If we are to get the money we need to carry on the great program of service set before us, some of us must give more than our share. After we have paid our part of the General Budget, we shall have to do more, for all cannot or will not do their portion. I know there are many people who can and will give the Lord an extra ox. There are many districts, churches, missionary societies, young people's societies, Sunday schools and individuals that will want to hang a pretty cow tail on the Lord's calabash. Of course we cannot do this until we have paid our General Budget. But when we have met our full obligations, we are free to make the Lord as full and as free a gift as we choose. The heavens only are the limit. I know, too, that tomorrow, when these people go to the King for help, He will remember those cow tails and will not keep the petitioners waiting long. Many favors will be showered upon the people who hang cow tails on the King's calabash by means of their special, freewill offerings.

And now, lastly, we must kill the black bull. There is a hard battle to be fought and won. King Jesus, having come out among His people, calls to every member of the church, "Here it is, Nazarenes." Let every one of us lay hold wherever we can get a grip. Let us go or send. Let us build or pay. Let us sacrifice, work, preach, and push. Let us make it "the whole business of the whole church to give the whole gospel to the whole world."

B. PREPARATION FOR FOREIGN MISSIONARY SERVICE

I heard the voice of the Lord saying, Whom shall I send, and who will go for us? Then said I, here am I, send me (Isaiah 6:8).

A call to service is usually a call to prepare for service, for there are not many cases in which the person called is really prepared for the work he is called to do. Experience shows that people who have made the work of the foreign missionary their life's calling, have usually felt their designation to this task under the influence of parents and pastors, rather than under the influence of special missionary speakers, and a surprising number of them have been called while yet in high school or in the first years of college.

And since in these days several years of specialized preparation are required, it is increasingly important that parents, pastors and all church leaders who have to do with high school and college age groups acquaint themselves with the standards of requirements expected of those whom the church will designate for its representatives in the lands beyond the seas. Also, these general standards should be kept before our children and youth that they may know and realize what is expected of them if they are to hear and heed the call to be foreign missionaries.

Among the essential qualifications and indispensable characteristics of successful foreign missionary candidates, we list the following:

1. *Spiritual Qualifications*

a) Missionaries and missionary leaders of all denominations have agreed that a definite knowledge of God is of first importance in missionary qualification. Describing this requirement in our own words, we say the prospective missionary must know he has been born again and sanctified wholly. He must know the joy of sins forgiven, and have the assurance that his heart is cleansed from all inbred sin. There is a divine response to the prayer of the seeking soul that satisfies and assures.

Sometimes people have argued that a "sinning, repenting professor" in this country will become an established Christian as soon as he crosses the ocean and lands in the field to which he is called. But experience does not justify this assumption. People who wobble here will wobble even more over there where they have fewer human helps. And when one reaches a foreign land and comes into contact with demon possession and heathen powers he needs to know by true and tried experience that the blood of Jesus can make the vilest sinner clean. Our church, thank God, stands for the second work of grace by means of which the truly regenerated are sanctified and empowered by the Holy Spirit for service. There must be no lack of clearness in doctrine on this subject, and no want of assurance in experience on the part of our missionaries.

During the trying days when the new missionary is struggling with a difficult foreign language, seeking to become adjusted to his new surroundings, trying to help tottering, newly converted nationals, and making his first attempts to lead the heathen to Christ he will need to know every day and all the time that the grace of God does keep him clean and enable him to stand.

b) The prospective missionary should be conscious of a definite call to the missionary task, and should be clear in the conviction that God wants him in the field to which he goes. And this certainty of a call should apply to missionary wives, as well as to missionary husbands, and to missionaries who go out unmarried to serve on the foreign field.

There are so many hard experiences, so many abnormalities, and so many disappointments in the missionary's life, especially in the first months and years of it, that the missionary needs to know and be assured that God sent him. And, knowing this, he will be able to draw on God for grace and strength to keep and make of him an overcomer.

c) The prospective missionary should learn by experience how to pray and to get answers from God. He should learn to win souls right here in America. One who is not willing to prove himself in this way should not send his application to become a foreign missionary. No district, church or individual should urge the appointment of a missionary candidate who does not give evidence of attainment in all these spiritual qualifications.

2. *Adaptability*

The missionary must learn to change, and he needs to be able to change quickly. John B. Culpepper used to tell of the old "Hardshell" Baptist who discovered right in the middle of the Sunday morning service that he had one of his socks on wrong side out. Without a moment's hesitation, he proceeded to take off his shoe and change that sock. His explanation was, "When I find out I'm wrong, I change right then and there." The missionary needs to be like that. He will be associated with members of his own race, as well as of the people he goes to serve. These people of both

and of all races have ways of living that differ from
those with which the missionary is familiar. Their
rules of courtesy and methods of expression will often
baffle him. But the missionary must, like Paul, "become all things to all men, that he may by all means
win some." He must look for the admirable qualities
in people, and when no moral issue is involved, must
seek to adapt himself to his new field and to its people.

I have known a man who was a wonderful trades-
man, and industrious beyond the average, but he
could not work with another his equal. He was a one
man organization, and when another came on the job
there was trouble until one or the other quit. Christian workers are like that sometimes. They work
hard, but will not co-operate with other workers.
They resent supervision and account all criticism as
unfriendly. The person in this country who does not
live and work harmoniously and efficiently with
family, friends, and fellow workers, students, teachers and others will not make it as a foreign missionary
and should not be appointed to the field.

My father had a beautiful bay horse which was
gentle and playful, and a great favorite with us children. He pulled the wagon or plow so long as he
wanted to work. But when he became tired or upset,
he would stand still, hump up his back, brace his feet,
and refuse to budge. You could pet him, beat him,
coax him, pull him, push him, but it was all to no
avail. He not only remained unmovable, but he kept

the other horse and the wagon stuck in the mud or
stalled on the hillside.

There are people also who will play so long as
things go their own way. But when they are denied
a location or office they coveted, or when someone else
is given something they desired, or when the conditions of the work are not to their liking, they just
stand still and block the work of others.

The mission field must have men and women who
can be sent alone or along with others. They must be
willing to either lead or to follow the lead of others.
They must take meager equipment and undertake
difficult tasks. They must often pull the wagon while
others ride—and even drag their feet. Missionaries
must be adaptable.

3. *Leadership*

The missionaries of today and tomorrow must be
well-trained. They must have high school and college
as basic training, and beyond these must have specialized training and experience.

a) Those who are to work in the medical division
must be fully qualified doctors or nurses, and with as
much practical experience as possible. On our better
developed fields the pioneer stage, when First Aid
training enabled one to serve as a medical missionary,
has passed. Medical missions presents one of the greatest responsibilities and one of the best opportunities
for winning souls to Christ. And for this task we must
have fully qualified doctors and nurses.

b) Those who are designed for the Educational Division must be well-trained preachers and well-trained and certified educators. Mission schools are usually under government supervision, and our missionary teachers must be able to meet and plan with government representatives and with the educators of other denominations. These educational missionaries must have specialized advanced training in university or normal to qualify for their task. Generally industrial subjects form a major part of the curriculum in the mission school, and people who serve here must have ability and training for both execution and instruction.

c) Those who go to devote their time to evangelism must have heart experience and burning zeal for the task. They must be able to give an answer to those who demand a reason for the hope they have within themselves. They must be well-grounded in Bible knowledge and in the doctrines of our holy Christianity, and be trained and prepared to impart this knowledge to others. The primitive Christian expects his missionary to know his Bible. He expects him to be able to answer questions. And he expects him to be an example in life, in experience, in testimony, and in devotion to study and to the work assigned him to do.

d) In addition to his general and special training, the missionary should know something about carpentry and building, for in all probability he will have to supervise the building of homes, schoolhouses and chapels, and will have to direct the repairing of such buildings. He ought to know a lot about agriculture, for he may be expected to supervise the fields, gardens, orchards, direct in the care of livestock, repair the farm machinery, make the gas engines go, and do just about everything the average farmer has to do or have done. He should be able to keep legible and accurate accounts of the money he receives and expends. And if the missionary is a woman, she should know something about gardening, sewing, housewifery, basketry, etc. Then there is also need for a few printers and men and women of strictly business training.

4. *Personal Characteristics*

a) Missionary candidates must be physically fit. It is expensive and unwise to send or try to keep sick people in foreign service. Workers there are always too few to make it possible for them to take on the added care of a sick missionary. Then, too, transportation and hospitalization are too expensive and too difficult to obtain. People who would be missionaries must be in good health, and they must be willing to pay the price for keeping good health.

b) John Wesley said, "Cleanliness is next to godliness." The spiritual leader must be clean in personal habits. Nothing is more out of harmony with the purpose of a mission station than dirt and disorder. Missionary candidates must learn to be clean and orderly in all the habits of their lives. A disordered house or room is certain index to a poorly disciplined personality.

c) Self-control is an indispensable characteristic in the missionary. Primitive people are great observers. They read the missionary as literate people would read a book. If there is anything wrong with the missionary, the national knows it. If the missionary is unfair, if he is wanting in the manifestation of love, if he is selfish or if he is inclined to take advantage, the national knows it without anyone's telling him. But if the national reads fairness, self-control, perfect love, and unselfishness in his missionary, he will then accept reproof and correction as from a devoted friend.

d) A sense of humor is important in the missionary. There is so much that is sordid and commonplace, that the missionary is likely to become morbid if he is unable to see the funny side of things. On the mission field, and in just the most ordinary things of the passing day, anything can happen, but a big smile and a hearty laugh gets the missionary out of many a desperate circumstance.

The list here given is in no sense complete, but it is enough to start us to thinking. When the call of God to foreign service comes to the young man or young woman, it is then time for him to examine himself and see wherein he is lacking. And, furthermore, it is time for him to set himself to the task of as fully as possible preparing himself for the noblest calling God has ever given to man.

During my grandmother's last illness she carried a great burden for lost souls. Even on the day she died she muttered prayers for the unsaved. She would call out, "There are so many broken hearts reaching out their hands for help." Then she would call my father and say, "Joseph, what are we going to do about it?" Tonight there are so many broken hearts in heathen darkness reaching out their hands for help. I, too, ask you, in Jesus' name, young man, young woman, what are you going to do about it?

C. OUT OF AFRICA EVER SOMETHING NEW

Say not ye, There are yet four months, and then cometh harvest? behold, I say unto you, lift up your eyes, and look on the fields; for they are white already to harvest (John 4: 35).

There is an old Greek proverb that says, "Out of Africa ever something new." They tell us that in three thousand years Africa has never failed to furnish proof of this proverb. Today many tremendous things are rolling into view from Africa. The most interesting of all is the African himself. It is as if a great tidal wave has swept over the whole country; lifting to the world's view from her valleys, jungles, swamps, grasslands and high plateaus Africa's 150 millions of people; and then as though the receding wave left the whole nation uprooted, adrift and dumped into the lap of the Christian world.

In no place in the world can be found the mixture of the very old and the very new as in Africa. We see

it in the dwellings: a modern, well-equipped home
within a stone's throw of little grass and mud huts in
which women dress in skins, grind meal on stones and
cook in earthen pots on open fires. We see it in their
means of travel: down the streets of almost any
village may be seen the skin dressed natives from the
country districts, the man walking ahead, the woman
following along behind with a sack of corn on her
head and a big baby strapped on her back. You will
see also the little burro moving along by the side of the
white farmer's span of sixteen oxen that move lazily
down the middle of the street, while behind, with
much honking for room to pass, comes a well-dressed
man in an automobile of latest model. You see it in
the people themselves: you may see a Swazi woman,
dressed in cow skins, hair mudded and greased and
piled high, and decorated with bright-colored mud
and porcupine quills; her neck, waist and body tied
about with charms she has obtained from the medicine man to protect herself from witches and sorcerers.
This woman may be talking to her son who is dressed
in European clothes. He is a model of neatness and
courtesy. If you address him, he will answer you in
perfect English, and he can discuss politics and war
and world affairs with intelligence. He is a qualified
Christian teacher, loved and respected by both natives
and whites. If you should meet the king of Swaziland
in Johannesburg, he would be traveling in a car,
wearing European clothes and speaking English. But
if you should get a glimpse of him at the royal kraal

in Swaziland, you would probably find him wrapped in a leopard skin, decorated with feathers, cow tails and beads. In some parts of the country parents still live who were once cannibals who cooked and ate their slain enemies, but their children are running steamboats, railway trains or working as government officials. Even today there are fathers who are witch doctors, smelling out witches, making "strong medicine" with parts of the human body with which to treat fields and persons: but their sons are fully qualified medical doctors, examining blood smears and parasites in hospitals and laboratories to determine the cause of their people's illness. The native men who used the first wheelbarrows in the Congo, having never seen a wheel, hoisted the loaded barrows to their heads and carried them to be dumped. Yet their sons are assembling transport planes and driving trucks. It has been said of Africa, "Never before in the history of the world has so primitive a people in so large an area had the full weight of so advanced civilization put upon them in so short a time." The whole impact came in a single lifetime. The normal development of a thousand years has been crammed upon Africa in fifty years.

In 1880, just 999 days after Stanley left Zanzibar, he arrived at the west coast, having finished his trail across Africa. The bleached bones of all the other white men, and over half of the native men, were left along that trail. Three years later, just 62 years ago now, the European nations began to realize Africa's worth and jumped at her, and divided her into 38 pieces, each one grabbing as much as possible.

Africa has almost the world's supply of diamonds, a large per cent of the gold, the largest known source of copper, 65 per cent of the cocoa and chocolate, nearly all the radium, and untold riches in ivory, rubber, cobalt, palm oil, wattle bark, etc. Africa stands rich, desirable, exploitable before a greedy world. She has been a source of the fiercest conflicts and of continual territorial, economic and political contention. The African in this process has been robbed and exploited. Not only was his land partitioned among outsiders who came with guns and gin, but he himself was made to supply all the cheap labor needed to develop the great farms and mines. Millions of native men, after a period of labor for the white man, come back to their native lands for rest, bringing with them samples of the white man's liquor, cigarettes, profanity, distinctive diseases and loose morals. The African feels confused and resentful. His religious and social life has been disrupted. All the best of his land has been taken away from him. In many places he has been put into the "reserve" which often has the worst kind of climate, and is of insufficient size and poor in quality. Taxation has been used as a means of forcing him to work in European enterprises. He is handicapped everywhere by color bar, by pass laws and by poverty. He cannot understand the white man, and he resents him.

The Christian Church is almost the only agency which might think of Africa and the African objectively and impartially, and the Church is Africa's special debtor. It was the so-called Christian nations that laid a heavy hand on Negro Africa in just those areas where she gave most promise of developing and spreading a higher culture. Her slavers came along the African coast from Dakar to the Congo with shiploads of rum, and left with cargoes of slaves, some of the victims being intelligent and kingly, from homes of wealth and splendor. Many of these slaves were brought to the United States. For each one hundred that survived the trip, four hundred are said to have perished in the "middle passage," and this does not take into account the terrific death toll of the slave raids or of the breaking in periods on the plantations. During the three hundred years of the slave trade, 100 million people were torn from their African homes. Whole areas were depopulated, while both the native and the white nations were debased together.

The African is naturally a religious being. He is in the world to stay. He has a joy of life and a will to live. His religion directs and controls every phase of his life. He is Africa's most glittering diamond, her most priceless treasure—her black gold. His spiritual qualities and capacities are worth infinitely more to the world than Africa's wealth of soil and mines.

Considering the African's ability to leap that chasm a thousand years deep in a single generation, interested people must ask, "What will come out of

Africa in the next generation?" This question the Christian world must answer. For if we will give them Christ, Christianity will replace animism; raw life and primitive customs will be transformed, and Africa's contribution will be good.

The Church of the Nazarene, along with other Christian denominations, has had share in a bountiful harvest. When I left Africa at the end of 1940, we had work in three provinces: Transvaal, Gazaland and Swaziland. Every main station, except Johannesburg, had a dispensary, a growing Sunday school, a day school, a boarding school and a farm on which much of the food for the natives was raised. Each main station works the surrounding district, and cares for the outstations of its section. Camp meetings are held in which people find God, and in which native Christians learn about the doctrines and institutions of the church. A great portion of our people are tithers. Most of them—men, women and children—are members of the Missionary Society and diligently pay their dues. Our African church is fast moving toward self-support and self-government.

In the city of Johannesburg and along the Reef, we have a splendid work among the 750,000 men who come there from all parts of Africa to work in the gold mines. We have 78 places of worship with over 500 church members. We have one missionary home, and two couples of missionaries are stationed in this section. We have scarcely touched the fringe of this great work. There is no place with greater possibilities than these compounds where the men are housed, the hospitals where the sick and wounded are cared for, and the "locations" where some 100,000 natives have permanent homes. If we can give these Compound men an experiential knowledge of salvation through Jesus Christ, they will carry the gospel story back to every part of Africa, and tell it around the campfires at night until men and women will believe on Him and be saved.

At Acornhoek, Transvaal, we have six missionaries stationed at the present time. We have a very efficient European nurse in a new dispensary building doing a remarkable work, a growing church, a Girls' Home and a big day school. This is a great bushveld country with tremendous possibilities among its 90,000 people. We now have five outstations, and 200 converts. We need many new buildings and much more equipment at this place.

In Gazaland, Portuguese East Africa, our opportunities are limitless among the many Shangaan people. Here is located our big Tavane Station with its schools and dispensary and a very large district work, which God has blessed very remarkably in the last few years. There are 53 outstation churches, 64 national workers, 1,800 church members, and 400 Nazarene children. There is a leper colony supervised from this station.

Swaziland is a small British Protectorate of 6,407 square miles, and with a population of 178,000 natives and 2,800 white people. About one-half belongs to the Swazies. White ranchers own the other half. Over 7,000 native men go yearly to the gold mines at Johannesburg. Most of them go to earn money to pay their taxes. The Church of the Nazarene works the northern half of the Protectorate. This portion is sparsely populated by rural people.

Schmelzenbach Memorial Station (Endingeni) is the place where Brother Harmon Schmelzenbach first planted our church in Africa. A big tabernacle building now stands over the place where Brother Schmelzenbach died, and near by his body is buried under a slab, a mute testimony of a work yet unfinished. This is the place where I labored for seventeen years, and where the Girls' Home is located. We have a beautiful station. The buildings are made of good burned brick, pointed with cement and roofed with corrugated iron. We have here boarding and industrial schools, and Miss Irene Jester supervises the big farm and orchards and keeps the place in good repair. The outlying district is large and beautiful. There is also a dispensary at Pigg's Peak, as well as at Endingeni, both of which are staffed with a European nurse and native nurses. The doctor visits these dispensaries once a month. The dispensaries care for the sick of the surrounding district. Thousands of people are contacted every year by those two busy dispensaries. There are 18 outstation churches and schools, 1,050 converts, 50 national workers and 700 children. This is our oldest district. It is well advanced, and is very fruitful and encouraging. Over 2,000 natives come to the great camp meeting here every year.

At Stegi our Bible School is located. Miss Ora Lovelace has been greatly used of God in the building of this training school in preparing workers for our fields. Let us not forget to pray for this school with its great possibilities. This station has a farm of over three hundred acres of rich land. With proper farming facilities and equipment, this farm would produce more food than the boarding students require. We have a good day school, a large dispensary which cares for a populous community, and six outstation churches in the surrounding territory.

Raleigh Fitkin Memorial Station—the place Dr. Hynd has made—at Bremersdorp, is well planned, in a good location and has many large buildings. Our big hospital with its staff of sanctified doctors, nurses and national helpers, cares annually for about 1,600 inpatients and 16,000 outpatients. It has a maternity and child welfare division, an orphanage and a School of Nursing and Midwifery. Our printing department is also on this station, and besides the regular school, we have here a Teachers' Training and Practice School. There are 13 missionaries, some associate missionaries, 26 national workers, eight outstation churches, 400 converts and about 250 children in this district.

A White Paper issued by the British Colonial Office of London, in 1944, entitled "Mass Education of Africa," deals with a policy for making all Africans, young and adult, literate during the next ten or twenty years. This policy is an attempt to make the whole population, Christian and non-Christian, literate within the lifetime of many of us now living. The Colonial Government has even now put into operation in Swaziland a million-dollar land settlement scheme. The Swazi government has secured over 362,000 acres of land. This has been surveyed and divided into small farms. The plan is to settle 25,000 Swazies on these huge demonstration plots, where the latest agricultural methods, with modern equipment, under strict supervision will be used. Plans for the expenditure of other large sums of money for the economic development of the country are being considered.

Will all these plans for economic, social and political advancement end in secular materialism? Can the Church of God provide the men and money required to maintain an equivalent spiritual advance in the whole of Africa? The Church of the Nazarene has a splendid start on her part of the field. With our great forward program calling for the raising of a million dollars for missions each year, and five hundred new missionaries during the quadrennium, let us send scores of new workers to Africa. Let us train and equip hundreds of national workers. Let us build the long needed buildings, properly equip our stations, open new fields, walk in at every open door, produce the quantities of reading material demanded by the education of the masses, and in every way—hand, head and heart—give Africa a chance at the gospel of Christ which "is the power of God unto salvation to every one that believeth."

Up in the high mountain a heathen man lay dying. Every morning early he would rise from his stupor, and cry into the darkness, "Haven't they come yet?" The mother, thinking him delirious, tried to comfort him by telling him to rest, for the greatest witch doctor in the neighborhood was mixing strong medicine to take away the evil that someone had placed upon him. He could not rest, and after hearing his cries for many nights, the mother asked, "Haven't who come yet?" He answered, "The people of God. Haven't they come yet to tell me about Jesus? I am dying alone in the darkness." His little sister who also heard his pitiful pleadings, took it upon herself to fetch the people of God. She came to the mission station in the afternoon and asked me if I would go and talk with her sick brother. By questioning her, I found that her brother had been to the mines, and was probably dying of tuberculosis. He lay there seemingly unconscious at times. But at the hour in the morning when the Christians used to arise to pray, he called for them to come and tell him about Jesus.

The distance was long, and the trail was new to me, so I told the little girl to run along home, and that when the sun came up over the hill in the morning, she would see me coming to pray with her sick brother. The child would not go, even though I kept telling her that the darkness would overtake her if she waited. Over and over she asked, "Will you come and pray with my brother?" I said again, "Tomorrow I will surely come." She began to weep. Great tears rolled down her cheeks and splashed on her naked chest, and she cried, "Not tomorrow, Daughter of the King. Come today. He won't be here tomorrow." I went immediately. We crawled into the little dark hut, passing the witch doctor who sat just inside the grass enclosure cooking his medicines. On an old mat in the middle of the floor lay a young man, seemingly lifeless. I thought I was too late. The little sister got on her knees, took the boy by the shoulders, began to shake him, and to call into his ear, "Wake up, brother. She has come. Wake up." His eyelids slowly opened. I shall never forget those eyes. It seemed as if those eyes had returned from the grave. Such longing, such misery, I have scarcely ever seen. I bent close over him and told him of the Saviour's love. The witch doctor came in and crawled on his knees around us. He had his medicine in his mouth and spit it on the floor, on the blanket, into the vessel of the boy's food. We were both doing our best—he to save the boy from the power of witches, and I to save his soul from hell. The expression on the boy's face changed. Misery gave place to hope. He tried to raise his right hand to indicate that he had chosen Christ, but the hand fell back lifeless upon the chest, and soon he was gone.

Millions in dark Africa cry out in the night, "Haven't they come yet? I am living and dying in darkness." And I would remind you in the words of that little girl, "Not tomorrow, child of God. He won't be here tomorrow." What we intend to do we must do today. The mountain may be steep, the way may be long. But there is yet time for us to reach them before the sun goes down.

D. If You Don't Like It Change It—Your Father Is Rich

What is that in thy hand? A rod (Exodus 4: 2).

What hast thou in the house? Not anything, save a pot of oil (II Kings 4: 2).

How many loaves have ye? A lad hath five barley loaves and two small fishes but what are they among so many? (Mark 6: 38; John 6: 9).

You will notice that these three questions are asked by the Lord or His representative. The answers are man's reply to God.

African tribal life is organized on a basis of collective possession. It suppresses individuality for the advancement of the tribe. It is a woman's duty to marry and bear children for the sake of the tribe. She is not a free agent in marriage, and love is not a necessary factor. In Swaziland marriage is in some cases an arrangement between two families. The girl, under this procedure, is not always consulted about the matter. Often a man gives a daughter to his creditor in payment for a debt. The man may be old and ugly. He may already have one or more wives. If a girl does not go willingly to the man who has been selected for her, in theory she is not supposed to

be driven; but in practice she is forced to go even
against her will. In the early days such unwilling
brides-to-be often fought, kicked and bit their brothers
who were given the task of making the delivery. Some
few escaped their hands and ran away. Others disappeared into the Transvaal where they found themselves friendless and alone. These almost always ended
up in the compounds, often diseased and living im-
moral lives. A few others, finding no other way to
escape, took their own lives rather than live a lifetime with men whom they feared or disliked.

A few years had passed since Brother Schmelzenbach had begun the work in Swaziland. One evening
when Mrs. Schmelzenbach was at home alone, a little
girl about fourteen years of age burst through the
kitchen door crying, "Hide me, Wife of the Missionary, hide me." It was little Ngobodhlane, one of the
first converts. She had been sold in infancy to an old
headman who already had six wives. While her
brother was on the way delivering her to her husband's
home, she had slipped away from him and had run
over the hill to the Mission. The girl was scarcely hidden in the storeroom when an angry voice demanded
at the door, "I want Ngobodhlane." Thus began a long
battle that finally ended in the girl coming to live with
the missionaries. They did not realize it that day, but
her coming was the beginning of the need for a home
for needy girls.

After the coming of Ngobodhlane others followed.
A gentle knock on the window, a cry in the night or

the sound of great confusion with many voices announced the coming of another girl in trouble. Some of them were covered with blood from head to foot. Some had great welts where whips had been unmercifully used. Others were bruised and swollen from being dragged and choked. When the girls were increased in number Miss Martin lived with them. She was not well in body, but even on her sick bed she agonized with God for those souls, and in all probability the big revival that came when I first moved to Endingeni was largely due to Miss Martin's prayers.

My first recollection of Brother Schmelzenbach is of a troubled man pacing up and down, talking about the problems that had come upon us because of these girls. He said if we could not provide better care and shelter for them, we might as well send them back to their parents.

In 1924 I went to Swaziland to our Annual Council and Camp Meeting. This was the year that Dr. George Sharpe of Scotland was our missionary superintendent. While Dr. Sharpe and Brother Schmelzenbach were talking over the problems of the work, and deciding where each missionary could do his or her best, I went to look over the mission station again. I kneeled before the door—a small round hole in the brick wall that separated the single workers kitchen from the girls' living quarters. I saw a small "L" shaped room. The dark antheap floors, the brown mud walls, with little windows near the ceiling enhanced by the gloom of the drizzling rain all made a

dismal picture. Sitting on the floor, her back to the
wall was a young heathen woman with great gashes
in her back and arms, and her clothes smeared with
blood. She was afraid, but she was determined and
sullen. Around about her were the hoes, boxes and
food of the thirty-two girls who made their home in
this one little room. It reminded me of a greatly
overcrowded chicken run on a very rainy day. I
walked around to the back of this building and there
in a hole, that extended perhaps six feet into the side
of a red clay bank, I saw four young women cooking in
a big black pot over a smoky open fire. This hole was
the only kitchen they had. There was no dining room
and no sanitary arrangements of any kind. I heaved
a sigh of relief, and thanked God with all my heart,
that I did not have to work at this place under such
horrible conditions. Just then I was called by the
stationing committee. Brother Schmelzenbach told
me they had been considering all the needs of the
work, that there was one department of special need
at this time, that they had prayerfully sought the will
of God and had decided that of all the available workers, I was the one most fitted to do this work. Then
they told me they wanted to station me at Endingeni
to mother these thirty-two girls. Had a bomb exploded
I could not have been any more shocked. Immediately
into my mind came all the impossibilities connected
with this work, as I had heard them discussed many
times. We were located on Native Area, and had little
security, so it would not be advisable to build perman-

ent buildings. Should we fall into disfavor we might
be forced to move away. But had we a place to build
we did not have money with which to build. At that
time missionaries lived in huts, and old corrugated
iron buildings. There was no possibility of the
church's supplying money for the Girls' Home. But,
perhaps worst of all, there was no building material
at that place. Lumber was prohibitive in price, and
roads almost impassable. Corrugated iron was too expensive and too hot. The clay of that region would
not burn for bricks, building sand for cement work
was lacking and stones would have to be hauled from
a distance. Remembering all this, I tried hard to convince them that they surely must be mistaken. I told
them that I never had been able to work in dirt and
confusion, and that I could see no way to make the
place any different. I ended by saying, "The whole
setup to me is most impossible. I just don't like it at
all." Dr. Sharpe waited until I had finished, and looking me in the eye, said, with force, "If you don't like
it, daughter, change it." I asked how this change was
to be made, and from where I would get my help. He
answered, "Your Father is rich." I went in before
these men free and hopeful and came out in less than
five minutes, having inherited a family of thirty-two
children. I felt burdened and depressed.

I could not forget those words, "If you don't like
it, change it. Your Father is rich," so before I finished
my moving, I decided that I would do my best to
change any changeable thing. I had scarcely got

settled in my new home when God sent one of the greatest revivals I have ever seen in all my life. There was no evangelist, little preaching, few altar calls and no program. We stayed day and night in the building without dismissal. People went and came as they desired. The whole building was an altar. People lay for hours in one spot on the grass covered floor, each one doing his own praying. At the close of the meeting not one was left hungry-hearted. One of the greatest reasons why I know that this was a very unusual outpouring from God is because after twenty years I find that of the number that sought God in that revival, twenty-nine later became national workers for our church. There were six preachers, three Bible women, two nurses, seven teachers and eleven preachers' wives. The revival season over, we found that, as is always the case when God mightily visits His people, many of our difficulties had disappeared and the remaining ones did not look so unsurmountable.

We decided to change the girls' living quarters. We dug a hole by the side of our house to expose the red clay with which we began to make green bricks. The girls carried water from the creek, in five gallon coal oil tins on their heads, and poured it in the hole. Others with their bare feet stamped the clay into the right consistency. I stood with some of the girls on a shelf-like place on one side of the hole, with the brick forms before us. Girls lifted the mud with their hands and put it by the side of the forms. We splashed it into the forms with force enough to fill all the corners, break the bubbles, and cover ourselves from head to foot in layers of mud. Other girls brought the empty forms, immersed them in a puddle of water by our side, sprinkled them with sand inside and out and slipped them into place before us. We slid the filled forms to one side where others grabbed them and ran to lay them in long rows in the sun to dry. We made thousands of green brick.

We could not find a trustworthy builder so, some of the schoolboys came to help us build. We tore down two sides of the girls' room, widened the place and made it much longer. We divided the inside into seven rooms and left a little hallway down the middle. We made three rooms about eight by ten feet on one side, and four smaller rooms on the other side. The hall was perhaps three feet wide. The partitions extended only to the top of our heads. The inside doors were merely holes in the wall, but each room had a little window too small and too high for anyone to easily crawl through. There was a small-sized door at the outer end of the hall. The other end opened into my quarters. We roofed our house with pieces of old corrugated iron on which we labored manfully trying to stop the many holes. White clay from the river decorated the top part of the walls and black tar the bottom. The floors were of antheap beaten hard with stones. When the building was complete we were proud of our home.

We called Mr. and Mrs. Schmelzenbach up to see our dream house before we moved in. He stood in that little hallway and wept, as he praised God for the beautiful home, telling us how he had hoped and prayed that God would give us just such a place. We all felt that night as if the New Jerusalem had indeed come down to earth at Endingeni. We moved in, five girls in a room. They were confused in such a large building for they had scarcely ever seen a native house with more than one round room. After this we built ourselves a kitchen and a nice big airy school-room of green bricks, and we fixed up another room for our dining and study room.

Time passed, new girls came nearly every week. One girl jumped into a raging torrent and crossed because God was with her. Another girl safely crossed a crocodile infested stream after a pitiful frightened prayer on the bank. Many girls slept in the open veld night after night, as they made their way toward the home God had provided for troubled Swazi girls. One girl walked over two hundred miles, making most of the journey by night, because she could no longer be a Christian and live at home. Only a native with his fear of spirits, darkness and death can understand the torture of being outside and alone during a long African night. I kept some of the girls in my bedroom, under the bed or in the corner behind soap box furniture for long periods of time until it was safe for them to live with the other girls.

Those were wonderful days in our little mud home. Many a soul found God in those seven rooms. Revivals were precipitated, demons cast out and bodies healed. God literally lived with us and found His opportunity in our extremity.

Sometimes we were able to make friends out of the pursuers of a girl and they would go home partially pacified when we promised that we would care for their girls as long as they stayed with us, if they ran away we would notify them, and if they got married we would not keep the dowry cattle. We did not make friends with all of them, however. We suffered many cursings and many long nights of fear, lest we be unable to protect the girls who came to us. In later years many of these one time enemies became some of our best friends. They saw that we loved their children, and that the ones who lived with us were not lost to the family. They often visited at our mission and were glad for the girls to come home and teach them the ways of Christ.

As our family increased, our home seemed to shrink. The roof was leaking badly. When it rained we ran for tubs and dishes. During nights of heavy storm the girls napped in relays, part of them bailing water while others squatted in rows around the edge of the room and used each other's shoulders as pillows. Then, too, disease seemed ever to be hunting us down. We used the kitchen where the food for the missionaries was cooked as the isolation ward. Often we would have as many as three patients lying on the floor in this little room, each one with a different contagious or infectious disease. I paced the floor for hours, many a night, begging God to protect us from

the pestilence of the land. I was always haunted lest
some disease break out upon us, and we lose many
girls in our crowded rooms, and find ourselves in difficulty with both the natives and the government.
Last, but not least, the sleeping space on the floor was
all used up. They slept ten in a room, the overflow
slept in the narrow hall. In the longer more narrow
rooms they slept spoon fashion, in the others they
slept half the heads pointing one way and half the
other way. They were so crowded that they could no
longer turn over at night, one girl independently of
the other girls. So one girl would call out, "Flop,"
and all the girls would turn at once. Sometimes it was
funny and sometimes it was not.

Then the day came when the chief sponsor sent a
girl to tell me that every available space in room and
hall was taken, and that if one more girl were admitted
to the home, in one room, they would have to sit up
during the night. I had spent many a sleepless night
asking God what I was going to do with these many
girls. One night I sat outside in the moonlight all
night, waiting on God. He wonderfully touched my
heart and encouraged me but I had not been able
to see any solution for this pressing need. I told the
girls we would have to stop admitting others some
day, and it might as well be that day. I had scarcely
sent this answer to them when a beautiful girl came
saying that she would not be safe at her home another night, so she had come to ask for a home with
the people of God. When I told her she could not stay,

she lifted up her voice and wailed. She said it could not be possible that the home God had given Swazi girls had now shut its doors in their faces; that many, many girls were comforted today by the knowledge that if the way got too hard in their own homes they had another home prepared for them by the Lord. She made such an impassioned plea for the Swazi girls that we could not turn her away, and so we took her in—the seventy-sixth girl of the home. She became a preacher's wife.

That night I went to the prayer hut to pray. The evening passed. God blessed my soul abundantly. I stood in the little hut in the darkness, my girls and my troubles forgotten and began to sing, "Riches in Glory." A thick fog seemed to come and cover the whole hillside upon which the mission station was built. Presently I saw a group of beautifully constructed buildings coming up out of the fog. Then I saw a great hand reach down and grasp these buildings. The fog disappeared and God's hand put those buildings right where they are today on the Endingeni Mission Station.

A voice spoke to me saying, "I am going to give you a mission station."

I said, "And it will take you, Lord, to build a mission station in this place."

The voice said, "I did not say I was going to build a mission station. I said I was going to give you a mission station. You are going to build the station." I quickly thought of all the seeming impossibilities—

the lack of money, of sand, of stones, of clay, and of my ignorance of building. I told the Lord how hard I had tried and failed all these years, and how very inadequate I was for such a task; then He said to me, "What is that in thy hand?"

I said, "A missionary's salary: forty-four dollars a month, Lord."

Then I remembered all my load of trouble because of the girls, and said, "Seventy-six girls, Lord, strung around my neck like millstones." Then God began to talk to me. I saw that the rod in the hand of Moses was merely a stick which he had cut from the mountain side. It seemed wholly inadequate for such a task as was assigned Moses until it turned into the rod of God. After that it was sufficient to do the task God gave him to do, and in the end to leave Moses in much better shape than he was in the beginning. Then He reminded me of the story of, "What hast thou in the house?"

The widow, it seemed, had forgotten those few drops of oil in her cruse, but the Lord chose to use what the widow had on hand. When she poured out her few drops of oil, it filled all her vessels. Those few drops were sufficient, not merely to redeem the sons, but "the rest" was enough to sustain her household after the debt was paid.

He talked to me about the little boy's lunch of five biscuits and two small fish. I seemed to see the hungry multitude and the troubled disciples. I heard Him asking, "How many loaves have ye?" They looked at the little lad, the only one who had remembered to bring any food. They took from him his little lunch and with it Jesus fed them all. I saw the disciples pick up the fragments and take them back to the child— twelve big baskets full of biscuits and fish.

Then other Bible stories came to my mind. In each the plan was the same. Somebody needed help. God came to help. In every case He used that which the person had in hand. Given into His hands it was always more than enough. There always remained the fragments and "the rest." Again I heard the question, "What hast thou in thy hand?"

"Seventy-six girls, Lord," I answered. That night I promised God that I, together with the girls, and anyone we could get to help us, would do our very best. He promised me that when we had done all that we possibly could do, He would show us what God could do. I came out from the hut in the morning and told the missionaries that I was going to begin to build a whole set of buildings on our mission station.

How to begin to build I did not know. Then I remembered that in America when the Christians did not know what to do, they took an offering. I thought, "We'll bring an offering." I knew that many of the girls had never possessed a coin in their lives. I called the girls and told them what God had given us to do, and how in America we always began with an offering. I told them to pray and ask God what they could give. I set a day for the offering. When the morning came we were all excited as we gathered in the school-room. I told them they could stand one by one and tell us what they would give toward the new buildings. A group of girls stood up: they had been to Pigg's Peak, secured a contract from the native police to furnish roofing grass for their houses, at twenty-five cents a bundle. They had secured the permission of a chief to cut this grass on his lands. They promised to cut twenty bundles each. They would have to carry them on their heads, one at a time, the more than twenty miles. That would give each girl five dollars for her offering.

Another group of girls who were not free to leave the station, said that, since we hired men during the holidays to plow and weed the gardens for twenty-five cents a day, they would do the same work better at eighteen cents a day, if we would allow them to do it. We consented and so they pledged five dollars each.

Lillian, one of our two teachers, said that since God had given her such good friends and a home, she needed nothing else, that if she might eat porridge with the schoolgirls we might take her year's wages (fifty dollars) and put it in the offering. Our other teacher, Willie Young, a mere lad gave fifty dollars—all his year's salary.

They gave about all they had: mats, goats, chickens and food. There was much weeping and shouting. When we counted the money and pledges we had over $500. Before the first buildings were completed, this same group of students and teachers gave us over $1,000 in cash.

God's hand had taken the buildings and placed them on the very spot where we were located, so we felt safe to begin our buildings there. The government later gave us a grant for the additional acreage on which the buildings are erected. We determined to prepare the building site. We had to dig up a grove of eucalypti stumps, and level the land so it would not require so many stones for the foundation. We began the first week in January. All the school children, the neighborhood Christians, and the missionaries dug stumps. It was the hottest month of the year but God tempered the weather for us so we could work steadily day after day.

Nobody will ever forget how old Emely, one of our grandmothers, said that God told her she could dig out one of those stumps. She worked faithfully on her stump several days and got it out all by herself.

We needed a bulldozer to level the land, instead we had a few shovels and picks and our hoes. Moving so much earth with our equipment was a long, hard, back-breaking task. We needed a truck to carry the earth, but we had three wheelbarrows, some five gallon kerosene tins and old pieces of corrugated iron. We worked at this job many weeks.

God gave us the hearts of all our neighbors round about, so they dropped in to help us. The old women would work until they were exhausted, and then they would sit in a line on the top of the bank, kick their bare heels in the soil, clap their hands, swing their bodies and sing. Their songs were Swazi praise songs. They praised the girls who always had the greatest part of the work to do, until everybody, no matter how tired, could not afford to show signs of weakening.

They praised the children until their little heels popped as they ran back and forth with their loads of earth. The small boys worked in groups, pulling big loads on large pieces of old iron roofing. When the load got heavy, they pulled together and chanted in unison something about being old men with long, long beards. I worked with the natives every day, digging the bank down, loading wheelbarrows for the men and stronger girls to roll away, filling tins to be carried on the heads of the girls and loading various other things that served as means of transport for the loose earth that was removed. When the place was finally leveled off we could scarcely come in and leave it, lest it vanish overnight. The girls chased each other up and down the large open space, while I sat on the bank in the moonlight and thanked God for His wonderful help.

We had just finished our leveling when typhoid fever swept into our midst. Thirty of our girls lay ill. Hosea, the precious girl who gave Jesus her dress in place of the tickey, went to be with the Lord. The doctor told us we should find a new spring of water. I sent a number of girls to dig in a low place near their cooking huts. I went down late in the afternoon to see if they had found water. In every hole they had found a layer of gravel a few feet under the surface, and underneath the gravel was a layer of gray clay.

We dug on down to find the ledge that seemed to be under the clay, but found instead a layer of coarse grained, sharp, beautiful, white building sand. We dug about and found it the same everywhere. We scooped it up in pans and ran to show the workers and the sick ones. We were tremendously excited. Here was the beginning of our building material. When we had needed sand the girls had gone to a small pool about a mile away from the station and with their hands scooped small amounts from the bottom of the pool, or at other times they had carried on their heads, from a distance of several miles enough sand to do a little bit of cement work. To find a pit of such perfect building sand buried a few feet under the ground, right close to our building site, where we could dig it out and carry it up easily, was indeed a gift straight from heaven.

Not another girl took typhoid fever. The sick ones began to improve rapidly, and were soon recovered. We understood why we had been smitten with typhoid fever, for this was one of the few diseases that would make us dig for new springs of water, and thus find the sand that God had hid there for us perhaps hundreds of years ago. We began to carry it up in great quantities. During the extensive building program on this station, we have used this pit of sand which seems to be like the widow's meal, always enough. We carried in finer flaked sand for the finishing of the cement work. I believe that although the sand now left in the pit is mixed with clay and harder to prepare yet there will be sufficient sharp sand to finish one building that still remains to be erected.

We had been looking for clay that would make a burned brick. Brother Schmelzenbach had sought for years for this clay and had never found it. We were sure, since we had found the sand, the clay too, must be somewhere about. After several months of futile hunting, I got three white men to come and look the place over. At last one made a beautiful brick that rang almost like a piece of steel. He had found one layer of clay that ran across the veld less than half a mile from the building site. He began to work with numbers of natives and soon the bricks were piled in thousands and burned. To this day we have never found, anywhere about Endingeni, another bit of clay, except this one layer, with which we can make burned bricks.

About the time we dug the eucalypti stumps, one of the native men saw a stone protruding from the ground, and digging about found that there were quite a number of wellshaped stones that were so broken that with a bit of shaping would make good looking foundation stones. This heartened us and the men and boys dragged in other stones from the mountain until we had a sufficient supply for the foundations of the first set of buildings.

We now had our building place prepared, our foundation stones, our sand ready for cement work,

and piles of fine country-made bricks ready for the
walls. We needed a builder. One night I saw what
looked to be an old tramp coming down the road. He
was limping and tired. He asked for food, and a place
to spend the night, saying he would work to pay his
lodging. I saw that his shoes were worn out and his
feet blistered, so I gave him money to go to the native
store and buy himself a pair of shoes. He said he was
a builder. I thought he had merely seen my building
preparations. He had never before worked for a
woman and he did not intend to begin. In the end he
decided that since I had been kind to him, he would
humble himself and work enough to pay for his food
and shoes. So, Peter Harrington, an Irishman trained
in England, a first class builder, worked for his shoes
and is today still working for the missionaries making
beautiful buildings for our church all over Swaziland.

Irish Peter loves three things: he loves to make
beautiful buildings, he loves to tramp, and he loves to
drink. His drinking makes it hard for him to work on
contracts in the cities. He told me that as he was
tramping along the road over in the Transvaal, many,
many miles from Endingeni, all of a sudden one day a
great urge came upon him to cross the mountains and
go into Swaziland. The white people urged him not to
attempt the long dangerous trail without a horse and a
guide. He had neither, and was broke. He had never
been to Swaziland, and had never before wanted to
go there. But now he felt as if he must go. He followed the trail up over the steep mountains, fording

the rivers, climbing the Devil's Stairway, crossing the Devil's Bridge, and walking into Endingeni. He passed two places where they were needing builders, but he passed them by, trudging right along until he arrived, shoes soleless and feet blistered, at our open door. God had provided Himself a builder. Had we searched all over Africa we could not have found a finer workman.

Peter, the natives call him "Long One," worked early and late for a reasonable wage, taking great delight in every building, and finishing for us, one of the best looking and most substantial sets of buildings in all Swaziland. When he gets drunk, as he often does, he tells how "me and God built the mission station." He says that Dulile (my native name) reckons it was God who put that urge into his heart to go to Swaziland. And indeed I know it was God bringing in the builder. Peter would work for months without drinking, and then go on such a spree that I would be forced to fire him and have somebody take him far away from us. But when he sobered up he would always come back. I needed him and would hire him again, and he was glad to work. There was nobody who could finish what Harrington began. I do pray that after all the years of wonderful service Peter has given us, his soul shall not be lost.

Our money was gone. We must have immediate help. I had told God that we would not go into debt. There were two white men and a few natives working for wages, and there was much material to be bought.

The money began to come. Nearly every letter had a small amount. One of the first weeks I received about $2,000. Of this one large donation was $500 from an old man in Colorado. He had put this sum away for his burial, but God told him to send it to Africa. This good friend is still alive today and is still serving God. Every month there was just enough to pay the bills. When it was nearing the time to buy the roof, we began to fast and pray and ask God to help us so we would not have to stop building.

Over in New England they were having an assembly. They began to take a missionary offering. Somebody suggested that they make it as large as they could, and send it to Louise and Fairy for their girls. That evening Brother Robert Clougher was walking down the street of the city in which the assembly was being held. God spoke to him and said, "I want you to go to the Assembly and put a check for $5,000 into the offering." Brother Clougher thought he must be mistaken, for he did not have that much money. But God said, "You know where you can get it." Convinced that God had spoken, he went to the place as directed and found them taking a missionary offering. One woman gave the money with which she had intended to buy an Easter hat; another gave the money she had put away for a new carpet. God said to Robert Clougher, "Here is where I need your money." He gave his check. The people were so electrified by this wonderful gift that they gave another $2,000.

In a few days we received a cable in Africa saying that they were sending the money. We ordered the roof, and by the time the bill came the money was there to pay for it. We did most of the painting, and all of the decorating ourselves. We dedicated our lovely Girls' Home, which we call Clougher Hall, and our beautiful missionary home, free of debt. These first two buildings cost over $14,000. There are many precious friends in America who labored faithfully with us until these buildings were completed. Foremost among them were the Lansdale, Pennsylvania, women and our long time friends in Colorado.

We dedicated these buildings in December, 1932. In February of the next year, while I was in the prayer hut praying, God told me that I was to build all the needed buildings on the station and that it was time to move forward again. We needed a large tabernacle very much. During the winter hundreds of natives would come up to our place for camp meeting. We would spend weeks making a grass and cornstalk tabernacle for this one meeting. The women and children would sleep in this building. They lay, in long rows, side by side, all over the grass covered ground. If it hadn't rained in weeks, it seemed that always at camp meeting time it would rain. The people would get drenched, take cold, and nearly every year some old or sick one would die from exposure.

Brother Schmelzenbach came home to America and went up and down the country telling of the need of a tabernacle. People promised to help, but somehow they soon forgot. He had gone on to his reward, and the crowds had increased. The last meeting we had in the grass tabernacle, a terrible storm reached us during the last service on Sunday night. Almost a thousand people were drenched to the skin, and we ran up and down all night like drowned rats waiting for the daylight that seemed never to come. It was during the depression. Money was very scarce, so when I began the tabernacle my faith at first reached only the foundation stage.

As we laid the stones deep and wide my faith began to grow. We started the brickmaking. Fairy gave me money to buy the windows so we decided to build the walls. Our African Missionary Society gave me money to buy the roof. I decided to finish everything but the cement work which would cost a lot of money. When it was time to think about cement, I received in one week, from many separate people, almost $2,000. So we finished the whole tabernacle right in the heart of depression, without once waiting on finances, and dedicated it free of debt. It is large enough to seat, Swazi fashion, fifteen hundred people.

After this we built the dispensary, school buildings, sheds and outstation churches in this same way. We always began with an offering from the people. Then they did free of charge everything that natives could well do. We found out that we could change many things along the building line by praying and working hard when God helped us. God never failed us. When we gave into His hands, all that we had, He made it enough to finish the job and left us with enough to begin another project.

We had been so busy building that at first we did not notice we were not winning as many souls as formerly. We began immediately to change that. We asked God to give us at our local church altar, by the end of the month ten seekers. He gave us eleven. The next quarter we asked for twenty-five new converts. That was the time of our first great Mothers' Day celebration. He gave us twenty-seven seekers. The next quarter we asked God to give us 150 souls. The girls said, "He will give us them." That was the time of the great revival when we won 153 souls, and a revival started from Endingeni that swept the whole church and gave us several hundred staunch converts.

There was another very remarkable thing about those times. We all grew by leaps and bounds in our Christian experience. I had never before known so much of God's presence. He talked to me plainly. Many times He saved the walls and the brick when they would have been washed away by the rain. I distinctly remember two such experiences. When we were still building with green bricks, we had the walls of our school building nearly completed, when a heavy storm overtook us. I knew it would wash them down, if we could not keep them covered. We fought the high wind until midnight, climbing up ladders, carrying big pieces of iron to cover the top of the walls, but as fast as we carried it up the wind whirled it down again. Finally, I told the men that the walls were God's walls, that He was abundantly able to save them if He wished, and that we would go home, pray and go to rest. In the morning the sun came out and the walls were standing uninjured.

Another time when we were building the big home, a great, black, rain cloud came quickly upon us. Our brickyard was full of thousands of bricks that would be ruined if we had a heavy rain. The girls and I were just out from the mud pit, and we were unusually tired. I ran to the men and asked if that cloud would pass us. They laughed at me, and shouted for me to run quickly for shelter. They dropped their hoes and ran. Another few minutes and the bricks would be gone. I ran and climbed up on the foundation of our new home, close to the brick field, looked up to God and prayed a desperate prayer. "Lord, do you remember what you promised me that day in the hut? You said that when we had done all we could do you would show us what God could do." Faith leaped up in my heart at the remembrance of how God had helped us. I found myself standing alone in the wind saying to the big black cloud, "You can't rain on my bricks." It did not rain. The men came back after awhile and said they never before had seen such a strange thing.

The native Christians seemed to be little concerned during this time with the things that ordinarily troubled them. The girls became mighty soldiers in battle. They would believe God for anything. They worked like Trojans and never complained. They prayed for every new need with as much faith as if the need had already been met. They learned to prevail in prayer and become mighty soul winners. In their childlike faith, they asked God for whatever they needed, and got it.

It was always amazing to me, and each time seemingly new, to see how God used such little people and such little things with which to do such magnificent work. He made so much out of the things we had in our hands, our houses, and our pockets. It never seemed big enough for anything so long as we had it, but somehow, with God, it was always enough. Then we grew richer as we gave. I lived in a hut, but moved into a home. My salary was used for the building, but I still had enough to care for a large family of needy children, and to keep the station and district work advancing. I had one mule, and then I got two, and then my Colorado friends bought me a Chevrolet car. The more I gave Him, the more He gave me. If I did not build buildings I did not get money, but as long as I kept building He always paid my bills. And this seemed to be so with all who worked with me in this building program.

If it should seem hard to believe that God talked to me and did all these wonderful things I have related, I offer as proof of my story, that fine set of buildings that now stands over in Swaziland on the very spot where, years before, it seemed so very impossible to build, because of lack of land, money, and material. The whole set is complete except the quarters for the boys. The money is now in Africa for that purpose. A small part of the Boys' Home is now completed, and as soon as building material can be secured, the last building of the set will be erected.

A second proof, is the fact that these girls, and many of these converts are today in their little corner of the Lord's vineyard changing for God hundreds of things they don't like. They have learned that their Father is rich, and when His child has done all he can do, the Father never fails to show His child what his God can do.

And moreover I feel that this principle will work anywhere for anybody. I have observed that: (1) Everywhere God always begins on the little or much people have in their hands, and that in God's hands, it always grows; (2) Christians can change things they don't like, anywhere, any time if it is for God's glory. It takes a lot of prayer and hard work, and it takes all your oil, but it can be done, and (3) we will not suffer by turning over our all to Him. There will be more oil, and more meal, and more fragments— even twelve baskets full. "If you don't like it, child of God, change it. Your Father is rich."

a South Blvd High
Faith Turner